TRANSFORMING SCHOOL LEADERSHIP
and MANAGEMENT

to Support
Student Learning
and Development

Comer Schools in Action
The 3-Volume Field Guide
Edward T. Joyner, James P. Comer, and Michael Ben-Avie, Editors

---

Six Pathways
to Healthy Child Development and Academic Success:
The Field Guide to Comer Schools in Action
James P. Comer, Edward T. Joyner, and Michael Ben-Avie, Editors

Transforming School Leadership and Management
to Support Student Learning and Development:
The Field Guide to Comer Schools in Action
Edward T. Joyner, Michael Ben-Avie, and James P. Comer, Editors

Dynamic Instructional Leadership
to Support Student Learning and Development:
The Field Guide to Comer Schools in Action
Edward T. Joyner, Michael Ben-Avie, and James P. Comer, Editors

Edward T. Joyner, Michael Ben-Avie, and James P. Comer, Editors

TRANSFORMING SCHOOL LEADERSHIP and MANAGEMENT

to Support Student Learning and Development

The Field Guide to Comer Schools in Action

CORWIN PRESS
A Sage Publications Company
Thousand Oaks, California

For information:

 Corwin Press, Inc.
A Sage Publications Company
2455 Teller Road
Thousand Oaks, California 91320
www.corwinpress.com

Sage Publications Ltd.
1 Oliver's Yard
55 City Road
London EC1Y 1SP
United Kingdom

Sage Publications India Pvt. Ltd.
B-42, Panchsheel Enclave
Post Box 4109
New Delhi 110–017 India

Printed in the United States of America

Library of Congress Cataloging-in-Publication Data

Joyner, Edward T.
   Transforming school leadership and management to support student learning and development:
The field guide to Comer schools in action / by Edward T. Joyner, Michael Ben-Avie, James P. Comer.
       p. cm.—(Comer schools in action)
   Includes bibliographical references and index.
   ISBN 1-4129-0510-9 (cloth)—ISBN 1-4129-0511-7 (pbk.)
   1. School improvement programs—United States. 2. School management teams—United States.
3. Child development—United States. 4. Comer, James P. 5. Yale School Development Program.
I. Ben-Avie, Michael. II.
Comer, James P. III. Title. IV. Series.

LB2822.82.J69 2004
371.2'00973—dc22   2004007197

This book is printed on acid-free paper.

Acquisitions Editor:	Faye Zucker
Editorial Assistant:	Stacy Wagner
Production Editors:	Kate Peterson and Diana Axelsen
Copy Editor:	Ruth Saavedra
Typesetter:	C&M Digitals (P) Ltd.
Indexer:	David Luljak
Cover Designer:	Michael Dubowe
Figure Illustrator:	Mark Saba, Med Media Group, Yale University School of Medicine

For Albert J. Solnit, M.D.
Director, Yale Child Study Center, 1966–1983

Contents

Foreword

James Comer and colleagues at the Yale School Development Program (SDP) have made an enormous difference in schools and school districts across the country over the past three decades. There is a wealth of knowledge, insight, strategies, and lessons contained within the range of experiences of SDP parents, community members, students, teachers, staff, principals, districts, and other leaders. The beauty of the *Comer Schools in Action* set is that its three volumes have now given us access to this wealth of knowledge and ideas in one place. This collection is of inestimable value.

The first book lays the foundation: child development = education. *Six Pathways to Healthy Child Development and Academic Success* establishes the mission and vision. What we have here is a fundamental agenda for social reform.

Dynamic Instructional Leadership to Support Student Learning and Development then shows the Comer Process in action, making it clear that we are talking about systemic reform. The elements of reform are clearly set forth: the role of schools and districts, the need for integrated planning and curriculum, the careful focus on implementation, how teamwork drives and sustains change, how school-university partnerships can be developed, and how assertive achievement-oriented leadership at the school and district levels is a system responsibility.

The third book, *Transforming School Leadership and Management to Support Student Learning and Development*, represents a complete guide for how to introduce and carry out the Comer Process. It shows us what is involved in making initial decisions, how to proceed through six essential steps in the planning process, and how to start and continue assessment and monitoring. All the key relationships are addressed, both inside and outside the school. An important chapter sets out the SDP implementation cycle chronologically, taking us through timelines and activities for planning, foundation building, transformation, institutionalization, and renewal.

All in all, the *Comer Schools in Action* trilogy gives us the entire essence of Comer's success and the lessons learned along the way. It is theoretical, practical, and filled with ideas and guidelines for action that integrate theory and practice. The Comer trilogy is a landmark contribution to the field of educational change.

—Michael Fullan
University of Toronto

Preface

This field guide and its two companion books in the *Comer Schools in Action: The 3-Volume Field Guide* are reflective of the wisdom of Dr. James P. Comer, of the staff at the Yale School Development Program (SDP), and of all the people in the hundreds of schools in communities throughout the United States and abroad who have embraced the Comer Schools movement. This volume is the collective representation of what we have learned from parents, children, teachers, administrators, community leaders, politicians, college professors, clergy, and members of the helping professions.

Because we believe that the practitioner is an expert, we have included the voices of people in the field as well as those in the ivory tower. We are all scholar-activists, and when we combine our efforts, pool our knowledge, and achieve one accord on what we want for our children, we cannot be defeated. We can create schools and communities that foster the development of ethical behavior in young people and challenge them to high academic standards.

Enough data have been collected and analyzed by some of our best education researchers to demonstrate that SDP is tried, tested, and true and that its effectiveness as a comprehensive school reform model meets "the highest standard of evidence" (Borman, Hewes, Overman, & Brown, 2003). This field guide will help you see the program through the eyes of the people who have made it work, as well as the people who designed it and continue to refine it.

This field guide is based on and expanded from training materials that we have field tested for decades. It is the first commercially published field guide by our organization. Because we are constantly searching for more ways to help children and the people who serve them, it will not be the last.

—Edward T. Joyner, Ed.D.
Executive Director, School Development Program

REFERENCE

Borman, G. D., Hewes, G. M., Overman, L. T., & Brown, S. (2003). Comprehensive school reform and student achievement: A meta-analysis. *Review of Educational Research, 73*(2), 125–230.

Acknowledgments

We extend our deepest appreciation to the district facilitators, superintendents, principals, school staff, parents, and students within the SDP network. We could not possibly list every individual who contributed to the success of SDP over the past 35 years. In *Dynamic Instructional Leadership to Support Student Learning and Development*, we acknowledge the winners of the Patrick Francis Daly Memorial Award for Excellence in Educational Leadership. In *Six Pathways to Healthy Child Development and Academic Success*, we acknowledge by name superintendents, university partners, board presidents, and staff at states' departments of education. We also acknowledge foundations and funders. In this book, we acknowledge by name facilitators and former SDP staff members:

Facilitators

Juan I. Alegria
Doug Anthony
Laura Barbee
Thomas Barclay
Mary Becker
Enomoyi Booker
Rich Bossard
Cleo Boswell
Cayth Brady
Karen K. Brown
Peggy Brown
Rodney L. Brown
Sandra Bullock
Shirel Byrd
Dr. Anna Chandler
Rose Chatman
Dr. Sara Cocolis
Sandra Collins
Michael Charles
Dr. Herman Clark
Jackie Clemons
Phyllis Shalewa Crowe
Charles Cutshall
Christine Czajka

Nancy Devine
Judy Diamond
Della Ezell
Layne Ferguson
Bea Fernandez
Sharon O'Grady Fink
Lorraine Flood
Jessye Franklin
Diane Gallina
Jeannette Gann
Jacqueline Gathers
Shelley Gaughan
Shirley Glass
Dr. Jennifer Gordon
Wanda Grant
Christopher Griffen
Sonya Hamilton
Eleanor Herndon
Paula Holmes
Haywood Homsley
Dr. Judy Hurt
Gloria Jackson
Sheila Jackson
Laura Johns

Cynthia Johnson
Sharon Johnson
Pamela Johnson-Betts
Kathy Jordan
Betty Joseph
Sherrie Joseph
Connie Kilgo
Pam Landry
Marlyn Lawrence
SuAnne Lawrence
Ken Lehman
Dr. Gretchen Lofland
Vivian Loseth
Dr. Eileen Maret
Lisa A. Marth
Minnie Mayes
Mary Mayrick
Molly McCloskey
Louise McKinney
Erma Mitchell
Michelle Adler Morrison
Chris O'Brien
Kathleen Osto
Dr. Larita Owens
Olivia Oxendine
Jennifer Patterson
Joyce Payne
Barbara Pellin
Gail Pinkney
Jeana Preston
Walter Pritchett
Dr. Wilhelmina Quick
Carol Ray

Bill Ritter
Beckie Roberts
Verdell Roberts
Liza Rodriguez
Evelyn Ruiz
Gerri Russo
Nereida Santa-Cruz
Loleta Sartin
Dr. Wahbah Sayegh
Ellen Sistare
Miranda Slade
Joy Smith
Warren Smith
Amanda Wright Stafford
Dr. Zollie Stevenson
Jan Stocklinski
George Talley
Vernita Terry
Dr. Joyce A. M.Thomas
Richard Tuck
Susan Vaughan
Dietria Wells
Janet Wheeler
Clairie White
Maritza White
Ora Wilkerson
Dr. Audrey M. Williams
Vivian Williamson-Johnson
Gwen Willis
Joyce Wiseman
Geneva Woodard
Victoria Woodley
Jose Zayas

Former SDP Staff

Dr. Angelique Arrington
Dr. Joanne Corbin
Dr. Sara Gebreyesus
Dr. Jonathon Gillette
Dr. Wendy Glasgow-Winters
Dr. Muriel Hamilton-Lee
Dr. Norris M. Haynes
Dr. Alexandra King
Dr. Robert Kranyik

Zannette Lewis
Edna Negron
Dr. Lystra Richardson
Cynthia Savo
Dr. David Squires
Barbara Stern
Charlene Vick
Dr. Ernest Washington
Dr. Darren Woodruff

Beverly Crowther and Linda Brouard contributed to the clarity of the text of the three volumes in this collection. We only hope that they regain the clarity of their vision in time for the next book.

Trudy Raschkind Steinfeld became a cherished member of SDP's "village" as an editorial consultant to *Rallying the Whole Village*. We are delighted that she joined us as a coauthor in this publication.

We would like to acknowledge the artistry of Mark Saba and his unwavering faith that we would indeed come to consensus regarding the posters and art that appear in the field guide.

Members of SDP's village have deepened their understanding of how to promote the learning and development of children by reading the books that Faye Zucker, executive editor, challenged us to write. Her enthusiasm sustained us and her caring for children inspired us.

Thanks to the editorial guidance of Kate Peterson the field guide is more readable and more helpful to parents and teachers. We especially appreciate her patience with us.

A special thanks to Diana Axelsen, senior Books Production editor. The field guide is truly beautiful.

We are grateful for Stacy Wagner's help.

We would like to acknowledge the hard work of copy editors Ruth Saavedra, Kristin Bergstad, and Carla Freeman.

We extend a special appreciation to Artemis Morris.

Every national SDP staff member, regardless of position, contributed to the development of this field guide and deserves our appreciation.

Publisher's Acknowledgments

Corwin Press extends its thanks to the following reviewers for their contributions to this work:

Michelle Barnea, Educational Consultant, Millburn, NJ

Dominic Belmonte, Golden Apple Foundation for Excellence in Teaching, Chicago, IL

Jo Ann Canales, Texas A & M University, Corpus Christi, TX

Robert Ricken, Educational Consultant, Lido Beach, NY

Mary M. Williams, University of San Diego, CA

About the Authors

Malcolm N. Adler is principal of George Washington School in Camden, New Jersey. In 2002, he received the Patrick Francis Daly Memorial Award for Excellence in Educational Leadership. He has been a Comer-trained principal since 1990 and co-chairperson for the New Jersey Network of Comer schools.

Michael Ben-Avie, Ph.D., directs the Impact Analysis and Strategies Group, which studies corporate, nonprofit, and government partnerships that promote youth development and student learning. He conducts national studies designed to evaluate the effectiveness of mentoring programs and psychological interventions on children's lifepaths. Dr. Ben-Avie has coedited books about the Yale School Development Program with James P. Comer, M.D., and colleagues, and has published numerous book chapters, articles, and reports on educational change initiatives, high schools, parent involvement, and the relationship between youth development and student learning.

William T. Brown, **Ph.D.,** is a clinical psychologist and a former NIMH Research Fellow with the Yale Child Study Center. Dr. Brown's primary clinical interests lie in serving minority, underserved, and marginalized youth and their families. His research interests involve investigating the relationships between psychological and social development and educational risk and resilience, and examining the impact of mental health and educational policy on young people's development and educational engagement.

Larry Dornell Burgess is principal of the Nellie Stone Johnson Community School, serving Grades K–8, in Minneapolis, Minnesota. His interest is in developing young minds to reach their full potential in life.

James P. Comer, M.D., is the founder and chairman of the Yale School Development Program, Maurice Falk Professor of Child Psychiatry at the Yale Child Study Center, and Associate Dean of the Yale University School of Medicine. He has published seven books, more than 35 chapters, over 400 articles in popular journals, and more than 100 articles in professional journals. He has served as a consultant, committee member, advisory board member, and trustee to numerous local, national, and international organizations serving children and youth. Dr. Comer has been the recipient of the John and Mary Markle Scholar in Academic Medicine Award, the Rockefeller Public Service Award, the Harold W. McGraw, Jr. Prize in Education, the Charles A. Dana Award for Pioneering Achievement in Education, the Heinz Award for Service to Humanity, and many other awards and honors, including 41 honorary degrees.

Shalewa Crowe, M.Ed., is a member of the Youth Guidance team of Comer facilitators serving Chicago elementary schools. She is a former administrator and teacher in a private Afrocentric elementary school and a trained reading specialist. Ms. Crowe believes that schools must be structured so that students can be taught in a supportive, engaging environment that encourages risk taking and decision making.

Everol Ennis, M.Ed., is a School Development Program implementation coordinator with a background in counseling psychology. He serves as the intake coordinator for SDP and is the director of the Youth Development Unit, which oversees the Comer Kids' Leadership Academy. He is interested in issues relating to effective teaming and problem solving. In addition, he is involved in various community and civic organizations whose goals are to impact the lives of youths.

Felicia D. Gil, Ph.D., is the principal of Charles R. Hadley Elementary School in Miami, Florida. Hadley has been a Comer school for the past nine years. The Comer Process has been instrumental in the school having been identified as one of the top 20 high-performing schools in the state of Florida for sustained academic achievement and best practices.

Jonathon H. Gillette, Ph.D., is the director of the Yale Teacher Preparation Program and member of the sociology department. He was formerly the director of professional development and consultation for the School Development Program.

Fred Hernández, Ed.D., is currently principal of the Commerce Middle School in Yonkers, New York. He successfully used the SDP model to remove an elementary school from the NYSED "SURR" process. He led a high school with the SDP principles and mechanisms to strategically represent the school as an "authentic workplace" for students to experience academic success. In 1998 he was honored with the Patrick Francis Daly Memorial Award for Excellence in Educational Leadership.

J. Patrick Howley, C.A.G.S., is the director of Teachers Helping Teachers and an implementation coordinator who specializes in human relations work such as team building, communication, and conflict resolution. He has been with the School Development Program for 13 years.

Sheila Jackson, head of the Prince George's County Comer Office in Maryland, has been with the program for 13 years. She began her work in schools as a volunteer parent actively involved in the education of her four children and was soon hired by the Comer office full time as a facilitator in 1994. Appointed Program Director in 1998 and currently designated as Human Resources Team Leader/Instructional Supervisor, Sheila supervises seven people in the Comer office as they facilitate Comer implementation in the district and provide services as one of the designated SDP Regional Training Centers.

Sherrie Berrien Joseph, M.S.W., is divisional director, Office of School Development Support and Intervention with the Detroit Public Schools. She has worked for more than 30 years in social services program planning and implementation. She has served as a social services and parent involvement specialist with Head Start, the public schools, and other human service organizations and churches in Atlanta, New York, New Jersey, and the Virgin Islands. Over the past 10 years, she has been closely involved with implementation of the School Development Program in New Jersey and Michigan, as both field consultant and Yale faculty member.

Edward T. Joyner, Ed.D., is the executive director of the Yale School Development Program. He served as SDP's first director of training, was the original designer of the SDP leadership development academies, and initiated university–public school partnerships to strengthen local school reform efforts. He is the architect of SDP's systemic initiative, which coordinates the work of the school board, central office, building staff, and the larger school community to create an optimal environment for teaching and learning throughout the school district. He currently oversees all of the operations of SDP and serves as the lead implementation coordinator for New York.

SuAnne Lawrence, M.A., L.C.S.W., is a project manager for the Chicago-based Youth Guidance Comer school network and serves as the Director of the Midwest Regional Training Center at that site. She holds a master's degree from the University of Chicago School of Social Service Administration. She has helped schools implement SDP in Virginia, Wisconsin, Minnesota, and Chicago.

Valerie Maholmes, Ph.D., has worked at the School Development Program for 10 years and is currently director of research and policy. Her areas of interest include examining the impact of school and classroom context on teachers' and students' sense of efficacy. She has served on the Board of Education for New Haven Public Schools and as chair of its Curriculum Committee.

Nora Martin, Ph.D., is professor at Eastern Michigan University and EMU coordinator for the Comer Schools and Families Initiative. She has been a professor in special education since 1967. Her areas of specialization include parental involvement and learning styles. She is an implementation consultant to the School Development Program.

Michelle Adler Morrison, M.S.W., L.C.S.W., has been involved with the Chicago Comer Process since its inception, serving as facilitator, trainer, consultant, supervisor, and program manager. She has expertise in systemic whole school change, capacity-building approaches to social service delivery in schools, child development, parent involvement, community schools, team building, and clinical supervision. She also serves as an associate faculty member of the Chicago Center for Family Health.

Miriam McLaughlin is an implementation coordinator for the School Development Program in North Carolina and South Carolina. Her areas of specialization include resiliency, parent involvement, and working with groups. She is the coauthor of a number of books and articles on health and education processes.

Gretchen Myhre, M.Ed., is a research associate working with Dr. Comer. Her background is in elementary education.

Trudy Raschkind Steinfeld is a consultant and researcher with the Impact Analysis and Strategies Group, Yale Child Study Center, and is an education staff developer and group facilitator. She is also a certified trainer of Neurolinguistic Programming (NLP) and a member of the training and therapy staff of The NLP Center of New York, in Manhattan, where she teaches NLP and Eriksonian hypnosis. Ms. Steinfeld is a coauthor of three chapters in *How Social and Emotional Development Add Up: Getting Results in Math and Science Education* (Teachers College Press, 2003).

Jan Stocklinski has dedicated over 18 years to the Comer School Development Program. She is currently a senior implementation coordinator. From 1985 to retirement in 2000, she directed the Comer office of the Prince George's County Public

School system in Maryland, where she served a total of 32 years. Her professional interests include school reform, parent and family involvement, child and adolescent growth and development, teaming, and effective practices, including effective use of communication skills. For 16 years she taught part-time in the graduate program at Western Maryland College (recently renamed McDaniel University).

Rebecca Stetson Werner, Ph.D., is a Postdoctoral Research Fellow at the University of Massachusetts, Boston. She earned her B.A. in psychology and English from Amherst College in 1994 and her Ph.D. in clinical developmental psychology in 2000 from Bryn Mawr College. She completed her research and clinical training at the Yale Child Study Center. Her research interests involve the social development of young children, specifically their social cognitive abilities and social behavior. She is particularly interested in the development of aggressive behavior in young children and the developmental pathways and correlates of aggression.

Introducing the Comer Process to the Faculty for the First Time

J. Patrick Howley and Michael Ben-Avie

Principals ask us how to present the Comer Process to their faculty. We tell them what J. Patrick Howley modeled for us. Pat, who is director of Adult Learning and Development at the School Development Program's national office at Yale, is a thoughtful, clear-spoken man who really listens. When he teaches communication skills to principals at a week-long training called Principals' Academy, he demonstrates a way of being peaceful and attentive at the same time. We've all been positively influenced by his style, which is an excellent style for principals to follow. Here is Pat, speaking as if he were a principal who is describing the Comer Process to the faculty in the first such meeting they've had. The questions the "teachers" ask in the dialogue that follows were offered by Michael Ben-Avie, Yale Child Study Center.

PRINCIPAL: I wanted to meet with you today as a faculty in a different way than we usually do because I just went to a training about what is called the Comer Process. It's named after James P. Comer, M.D., a child psychiatrist who is the associate dean of the School of Medicine at

Yale University. He has spent his whole adult life successfully reforming schools, and hundreds of schools all over the United States have transformed themselves using his process. Yale has a group called the School Development Program (SDP) and they conducted the training I went to.

The process is hard for me to define because it's still new to me, but I'm going to just talk about the whole process as I naively understand it in these early stages. And rather than just have me talk for an hour, I'd like to have a discussion. That's why I have us sitting in a circle for the first time. As large a group as we are, I still think that we can have a dialogue and toss around some of the ideas. So as I talk about this Comer Process, if you have some questions and concerns and objections to what I'm saying, I want you to raise those because they will get me thinking. And if we can't come up with an answer here, I can raise those same kinds of questions with the local SDP facilitator who has been assigned to help us implement the Comer Process, our university partners, or our mentors at the SDP's national office.

I want us to go into this together, rather than me seeing this as a good way to go and then forcing it down your throats with you saying, "Okay, he wants us to do this, so we'll do it." I'd rather have us really know what we're jumping into. You know, it's a little intimidating for me because what I've learned is that this process requires me to do less authoritative leading, less telling everybody, "This is what we're going to do." It's more give and take, with faculty members doing more of the leading and me doing some following. I'm not sure if I know how to do that all the time, so I'm going to be looking for a lot of your input. Right from the beginning, as I'm sharing this, if you have some questions and have your own comments, I'm going to welcome those. I'm going to try to be doing what I have now recognized as a different way of facilitating the development of a school.

TEACHER: I'm not quite sure what that means, facilitating—you know, all of these educational reforms have their own jargon. What do you mean?

PRINCIPAL: Well, to me facilitate means helping, so I want to help us work together in a new way rather than *direct* us to work together. In the past, what I might have done was to come in here and say, "Here is the School Development Program. Here's what we're going to do. This is when we're going to do it. This is how we're going to do it. This is why we're going to do it." And I wouldn't expect too much input from you. Instead, what I mean about facilitate is that we're going to help each other understand the task by asking some questions as you just did. If I don't know the answers, I'll tell you honestly that I don't know, and then I'll make the effort to find out what we need to know. So facilitating means that we're going to always try to help one another. We're going to help one another become more effective in helping children and in working with parents and with each other. We're going to be coming out of our classrooms more often and meeting and learning from each other— not only learning about teaching processes, but learning to be better teachers and learning to be better leaders.

TEACHER: Can we back up a bit? You said "more meetings." I feel we already have so many different committees, we have so much work, that sometimes I don't even have time to grade the students' papers because I'm in all these meetings. You want *more* meetings!?!

PRINCIPAL: The Comer Process actually builds in ways of helping us to become more effective in our meetings so that we eventually take less time and accomplish more. The process has a set of "guiding principles" to help us so that we don't blame each other, we hear one another out, so we make decisions by true consensus and we have some kind of general agreement about how to work in the most effective and healthful manner, so we're committed to saying, "I need you." I personally realize, more than ever, that I need the teachers. You realize you need me, I think. So we need each other. We're interdependent.

> Teacher: You said "more meetings." You want more meetings!?!
>
> Principal: The Comer Process actually builds in ways of helping us to become more effective in our meetings so that we eventually take less time and accomplish more.

TEACHER: Every year they ask us at our end-of-year faculty meetings, "What do you think we should do better? How should we improve?" And even though we speak up, nothing ever happens with our great ideas.

PRINCIPAL: Nothing ever happens, even though someone is supposed to take the next step? Is that what you're saying?

TEACHER: Yes.

PRINCIPAL: Who do you see . . .

TEACHER: You, the principal.

PRINCIPAL: Right, right. In this case, now, the change would be that, rather than *me* taking it to the next step, it's going to be *us* taking it to the next step. The reason that sometimes things don't get done is that I can't do it all. If we follow the Comer Process, I won't be expected to. Through our teams and our joint planning, we will share the decision making and the responsibility for action. One of the things that's changed in our society is that we've become more diverse, we communicate much more through voice mail, e-mail, the Internet. Everyone has more information to receive and give, and it's not appropriate or useful for one person to make all the decisions anymore. Think of it: Our country is a democracy, which means it's participative, but we really haven't lived that out in businesses or in schools. So you've spent all that time giving me the information and then nothing happens because either I don't have the time or I don't agree with you. But now the significant change is going to be that *if we don't agree with each other we'll work out a consensus at this table.* And we're going to make that decision within some boundaries. My role would be less that of saying, "We can't do this, we can do that because I feel that way." Instead I would be guiding you and saying, "Well, our state mandates are saying this and our board of education has these goals, so we can't go outside those goals, but within those frameworks, we have more autonomy to make decisions. All of us here." I have less freedom to just make decisions based on my personal whim.

Now you may ask, "Why is he going to do that?" The reason is that I've come to appreciate that you're as knowledgeable as I am about this school, about the students, the parents, the teachers, and the support staff. You have different knowledge, but it's just as valuable and just as important. So I have to listen to you more. I really have learned that. I want to hear more about what you have to say because I've learned that everyone's opinion is very important if we want to get a better picture of what's happening.

Before, I only carried my own picture in my head. As I've listened more, and that started to happen only recently, I've heard more teachers and more parents tell me things that I didn't even know. And when I sat down with students—maybe you've noticed: I've walked into the cafeteria and had lunch with them—I just ask them simple questions sometimes, and I find out the most amazing things. Like the fact that some students don't feel safe in the buses. I knew that intellectually, but I'm now hearing directly from students about it. That's become very powerful for me, very urgent, and I hope we'll find some way to act on it right away.

So I realized that perhaps you knew that more than I did, and I don't know if I was listening to you. You can give me the feedback on that. I mean, you already said, "Well, I gave some input and nothing ever came of it." I think that's one of the reasons why I want to go in this direction. I do want to listen more and then act on the input. One of the reasons is that I realize I can't do it alone anymore. Life is too complex. School systems are too complex for that.

TEACHER: I'm feeling—and I'm sorry to be so honest—I'm feeling skeptical. You said that you have a lot to learn and that we're going to learn together. How are we going to learn how to do it?

PRINCIPAL: Before I went to this training, I just didn't know that there was a method that was already well established and working well in hundreds of schools. Now, I'm relieved because we don't have to reinvent the wheel. Dr. Comer has talked about child development, and I realize that this is adult development as well. We'll always be in a learning process.

TEACHER: My experience with all these educational reform initiatives is that there's always a select few people who go to all these workshops and receive training and they come back excited, and then, after a while, it all fades away.

PRINCIPAL: If we create what is called a School Planning and Management Team, you could put the issue of staff development on the agenda. The SPMT could come to a consensus that we need to have training in the Comer Process for all the faculty. You wouldn't come to me. You would go to the School Planning and Management Team, and the team leader would help a discussion to take place in which we said, "This is what we need to do. People don't fully understand the Comer Process." You might say, as a next step, "Enough of our parents don't really understand this. We want to have parents serve on this team, and they don't even really know what this process is. Sometimes they work against us, and we need to help them understand what we're trying to do here." So if training or orienting parents became an agenda item and we decided that's what we needed to do, the team would decide to do it.

> The work of the teams is the business of the school.
>
> —Lester Young, Jr., former superintendent, Community School District 13, Brooklyn, NY

TEACHER: You used the word "feelings" before. I've heard that the Comer Process is this kind of touchy-feely thing, just self-esteem for the children. Nothing really serious.

PRINCIPAL: The Comer Process is serious because it touches people's emotions. When SDP's executive director hears the accusation that the Comer Process is touchy-feely, he responds: "Guilty as charged." And the Comer Process is serious. A recent meta-analysis of all the comprehensive school reform initiatives found that the Comer Process was one of only three initiatives that had the strongest evidence of effectiveness (Borman et al., 2003, p. 161). Furthermore, why talk about touchy-feely as if that were a bad thing? Feelings are an important part of growing up. How do you feel when certain things happen in this building? Well, you have some feelings, and you may talk to your spouse about those. That's being touchy-feely. I think there's a place for touchy-feely, but SDP demonstrates that that doesn't mean excluding academic development.

Also, in educational leadership, you see all kinds of different programs. Let me just talk about some of the significant differences between the Comer Process as I've learned it and other educational change initiatives. I have material right here that I'll distribute at the end of the meeting, and then we can have another meeting where we talk about some of the ideas in here.

From my three days of training, this is what I've learned: The Comer Process focuses on *child development.* Most other programs do not focus on children the way this program does. It focuses on adults working together in a way that many programs don't even mention. Sometimes people have seen this program as being only for children or only about psychological development; only for poor children or only for minority children; or they've seen it as a mental health program or an African American program. But I really saw during the training why it's called "school development." It's truly about developing the school. One part of it involves drawing up a *comprehensive school plan.* You could really call this the Comprehensive School Development Program. It's not just touchy-feely; it takes in every aspect of school life.

The Comer Process touches every aspect of school life because it provides us with a common language to talk about children and their behavior. Dr. Comer's metaphor of the six developmental pathways is a powerful way of organizing our observations about the students, regardless of setting. When talking with parents, it is especially helpful to use the metaphor of the developmental pathways because the language is descriptive and nonjudgmental. The pathways are also an effective framework for evaluating the purpose of each and every initiative that we have in our school.

One developmental pathway that Comer talks about is *cognitive development.* There are five others: *physical, social, language, emotional, and ethical.* And a major point that he made, being a psychiatrist, is that each of these pathways of development is interdependent. They need one another. Just imagine: If some event happened in your own life that was traumatic to you, it would be hard for you to come to work. I've had calls from teachers saying, "My child isn't feeling well. I have to bring her to the hospital." Even if the child doesn't have to stay in the hospital, even if they have someone to stay with their child, they're not emotionally prepared to come in and teach that day. Their problem is interfering with their ability to do cognitive work.

The cognitive and emotional are two different pathways, yet they interact powerfully. And how do both of them influence the way children develop language? That's what the SDP trainers are going to be teaching us, among other things. You know, the students are learning all kinds of things in different ways. As they go through the school, for example, how they're being treated by the custodian or the cafeteria workers makes them feel good or makes them feel bad. We have an obligation to pay attention to their ethical development as well: teaching them right from wrong in how they're treating and speaking to one another. When a fight breaks out in the classroom and students aren't treating each other right, that's interfering with their learning in the classroom. SDP is saying that we have to pay attention to more than just academics, more than just their cognitive development. However, you'll see when we talk about the comprehensive school plan that we're still going to pay close attention to their cognitive development.

TEACHER: I feel like you're taking us off the road to smell the daisies. You know that it doesn't make a difference how you feel about a test, the fact is that you perform well on the test regardless of what you're feeling like at that moment. Because if I had called you this morning and said, "I don't feel like working today," what would your response have been?

PRINCIPAL: You know what it would've been!

TEACHER: I know exactly what it would've been. Why should we let the children have this idea that emotions are important and that they could potentially interfere with their school work?

PRINCIPAL: I don't want to overemphasize this focus on emotions. And you know, if you said, "I don't feel like coming in," you know what my response would be. I would expect you to come to work. I think that should be the same response with children. If a child says, "I don't feel like taking this test," or "I don't feel like going to gym," I don't think this program is going to advocate giving in. So, I think either something I've said or something that you've heard about this program is suggesting that we'll be softer on the students than we are now.

TEACHER: Well, if a student really deserves a C, I don't want to give that student an A or a B because I'm afraid of hurting that student's self-esteem.

PRINCIPAL: I think you're absolutely right. In fact, do you know what has occurred to me as I'm listening to you? In some ways, this program may be harder on children, or at least it will create higher expectations than we've had in the past, because we'll not just be expecting the children to perform well academically. We'll be expecting them to perform better in their relationships with us and with other students and with their parents. So if I see behavior that's inappropriate, I would see it as our obligation to respond to that in some way, but in ways that are good and healthy for development. Now sometimes that will mean a consequence, but one of the things that you learn in child development is that sometimes it may not be the best course of action to be punitive. Sometimes the child needs to learn a lesson through learning about relationships.

I think this is going to lead to all of us expecting more of children. We're going to be expecting them to speak better because we'll be focusing on more ways to stimulate and reward language development. We're going to expect them to eat better and to take care of themselves physically because we'll be focusing on more ways to stimulate and reward positive decisions they make regarding their health and well-being. We're going to expect them to perform in the classroom, and we'll be helping to create new ways of teaching them. We're going to expect them to talk to one another about their relationships in ways that are healthy because we're going to be teaching them new ways to solve problems.

We don't do enough of that in our society, and that leads to violence. You see violence all over; every day you read about it in the paper. Right now, we expect children to work out their differences, but we haven't taught them specifically how to do that. With the Comer Process, we will be practicing specific skills with the children so that they'll come out of school knowing how. And in developing socially and psychologically, they will be supported cognitively. You know, this has been very helpful to me to have you even raise the question because now I understand that we will be expecting more of our children, not less.

It really means more work from all of us, not only from you. Hey, do you think I want to go to another meeting? But in the long run, if it's going to help me feel like I'm doing a better job, that's great. In the long run, it's better for the children and better for our society, and that's why we're here in the first place. Why just do my job and go home and feel like I'm not really making any major contribution? Even this first meeting has contributed to my learning by hearing some of your concerns.

TEACHER (head of the mathematics department): What does this mean for me? I feel very threatened here. I feel like you're introducing new structures, new teams, new committees, a new focus on emotions—and I understand that that's coming. What's going to be my role?

PRINCIPAL: You're going to decide that. As chairperson of your department, you've held many meetings to deal with the nitty-gritty, everyday decisions of the department, and those meetings are going to continue. As you point out, though, there will also be School Planning and Management Team meetings. Some department chairpersons will serve on the SPMT, but so will parents and support staff and teachers who are not department chairs. It will be a *more diverse, comprehensive group of our total school community*, including both school people and outside community members.

> Head of the mathematics department: I feel very threatened here. I feel like you're introducing new structures, new teams, new committees—and I understand that that's coming. What's going to be my role?

The decisions that group makes will be educational decisions. What you're not going to be deciding about are things like snow days. The superintendent is not going to call every teacher and say, "We're collaborating. What do you think? Should we have a snow day?" If an accident occurs on a bus, I may just make a unilateral decision that we're leaving school early today and that I'm not going to collaborate with anybody. I'm going to make that decision. So I'm not abdicating my responsibility for decision making when I need it, and you're not going to abdicate your responsibility or lose your privilege about decision making, either. Our typical department meetings will continue the same way they have.

One of the things that we will be doing is communicating more through the School Planning and Management Team. The SPMT, as I said, becomes more of a collaborative group, a consensus-reaching group, in which they're looking primarily at whole-school issues related to teaching and learning. I'm expanding what I mean by teaching and learning to mean not just cognitive development but all pathways of development. So, they'll be concerned about how your department supports that process. We'll also have a Student and Staff Support Team, which will be focused on global issues of development for children.

TEACHER: What does that mean?

PRINCIPAL: We would have meetings of the special education Planning and Placement Team where we refer students who are having difficulties, and those students then meet with our school psychologist to be tested and counseled. We have that kind of process built in. In a Comer Process Student and Staff Support Team, that leads to discussions about *prevention*. How do we prevent problems from occurring? For instance, suppose this school has some safety issues and we have children being physically hurt a number of times or being hurt in other ways, and we begin to see this as a pattern. We would look at the pattern and look at the global issue and say, "What decision can we make that will prevent this from occurring in the future?" And then the Student and Staff Support Team would take this to the SPMT, which would collaborate on an action plan, and the whole school would be involved in taking those preventive action steps.

TEACHER: Right now we have faculty meetings and we have PTA meetings, and these meetings are held at different times. When you were talking about the School Planning and Management Team, you were talking about parent representatives on this team. Will we still have separate faculty meetings and separate PTA meetings?

PRINCIPAL: Absolutely. We will still have our regular faculty meetings. I might change them to make them more like what we're doing now, a session where I give you information and then we discuss the issues, but we're going to continue with faculty meetings. The PTA will continue to meet. The role of the Parent Team will be to get more parents involved at many different levels. It is almost more a parent process than it is a parent team. *As more and more parents become involved, they increasingly feel that they're in a partnership with us.* Remember the incidents that we had a couple of years ago when parents attacked individual teachers verbally? The parents complained that the teachers didn't care. And what we talked about in the faculty room then was whether the parents cared. It occurred to me when I was in the Comer Process training that the parents don't see us as partners and we don't see them as partners, either.

If we can get more parents truly involved, when we have a concern, they'll call you. But they won't say, "Mr. Smith, how come you didn't do such and such?" They're starting to talk *with* you, and they're saying, "You know, I've had some trouble with my son at home and I wanted to just kind of check this out with you," and then, "Could we meet and talk some time?" And now you don't feel like you have to be defensive about what you're doing because they're really saying, "Let's just talk about our child"—*our* child.

> Principal: The PTA will continue to meet.

That's what I see the Comer Process being about and the parent process being about. That's where the guiding principle of *no-fault* is really felt. The parents feel that we're not blaming them, and we really feel the parents aren't blaming us. We're all willing to sit down and say, "Let's talk about this, share our ideas, and solve it." So I think we have some things to learn, and I think parents have some things to learn.

TEACHER: You used the word consensus several times. What do you mean by consensus?

PRINCIPAL: I don't know if I can describe consensus in just a few words, but when I looked it up I saw "general agreement." That doesn't necessarily mean that everyone agrees. But what it does mean is that even those people who have disagreed have really been heard. If I said to a person, "Have you felt like we have heard you on this team?" he or she would say, "I feel that people have heard my opposing point of view." Often, some parts of an individual idea can be merged into the group's idea so that several goals can be included in the final decision. The proposals can be blended, in other words. But if there is still opposition, the team leader could probably say to that person, "Okay, would you be willing to go along with this decision even though you disagree with it? Would you be willing to support it and let us try it out and see if it works? We may find out that you're indeed right, but I hope that you won't block it or just walk away because this decision is different from your opinion." And the person would say, "All right." That's what I mean by consensus: that we've all sat down together, and we've talked out all of the different viewpoints, and then we say, "Okay. We could talk about this forever, but if we talk about it forever, we'll be paralyzed."

So at some point, and I think this is the difficulty in this process, all of us are going to have to let go. I feel very strongly that I, in particular, am going to have a hard time with this, and this is where I say I have a lot to learn that you can teach me. I may want to say to you, "Hey, I'm the principal. Let me make the final decision here because I'm personally uncomfortable with your decision." And I'm beginning to learn that I don't have that right to do that anymore. I have the right and obligation as a professional to give my point of view, and you have the professional obligation to hear it, but the reverse is also true. I'm not solely in charge anymore. If we realize later on that there's a better way or a different way from the particular decision we reached by consensus, we'll review it and develop consensus on a new way to proceed. But the way I understand it, we'll be more open to trying things out.

Also, consensus does not mean that we're saying, "Eloise's idea is better," because then we're focusing on Eloise. Instead, we're focusing on ideas, and we're saying, "We see that more people are leaning in the direction of this idea rather than that idea. We've listened to two or three people who have objected, and we've given them every opportunity to explain their objections, yet almost all of us still prefer the first idea." I would say at this point in my knowledge, that the majority view would still constitute consensus. I would suggest at that point that we try out the idea preferred by the majority but assess it as we try it because *part of the Comer Process is action research. Let's continually assess it, and let's modify it if it's not working.* Let's not just say, "Okay, we agreed to it and come what may, we're going to go and do it." Later on, when you're giving input again and saying, "Look, I told you this wasn't going to work and I see it's not working here and here and here," the people who favored the consensus are not going to let their pride blind them to the results. This process opens it up to reassessment.

So I think that makes it harder for all of us in some ways, if you don't count how much better the outcomes are going to be. It's always been easier just to say, "We decided it. Let's do it. Let's not visit it and revisit it because that takes time and energy." Earlier, someone objected to more meetings. The reason for more meetings is to reassess and refine whenever we discover problems in a process or project we had decided on.

Now let me go back to the idea of more meetings because it seems like putting in more energy. Right? But what happened last year when we made a decision and then it didn't work and we didn't have a way to review it? I'll tell you what happened, because people told me. They had arguments in the hallways. You saw that. They had meetings after school, on their own, outside the building. And there were—these aren't my words—there were "complaining sessions." Right? People complained about it. Well, why were there complaining sessions? Because there was no vehicle, no process for them to bring it legitimately back in to say, "Here is what we're seeing. Here is a concern we have."

And they didn't come to me. Maybe that's because of my style. Maybe it's because I'm the principal. Maybe it's because in the past they perceived me as someone who was not going to do anything anyway or as someone who doesn't like decisions to be challenged. I think one of my problems is that I'm comfortable making decisions. That's why I became a principal. I want to make the decision and then get on with it, and I don't want to go back and hash it out again. But now I'm realizing that sometimes issues really need to be hashed out again. And what tells us that they need to be reexamined? If some parents are saying, "This is an issue" and some classroom teachers are saying, "This is an issue" and some support staff are saying, "Yes, this is an issue" then, by golly, it's an issue whether I want to admit it or not.

I am learning that I'd better listen to my—Wait. I don't want to say *my*. I want to listen to *our* group here. What I'm realizing is this isn't *my* school. This is really *our* school. It has to be *our* school. Because if I had to leave tomorrow and somebody else came in, you'd know more about this school than the new principal. And you know as much about the school as I do. It's ours, you know, and we've got to help each other. That's what this is all about.

I feel like I've done a lot of talking today. I'd like to give you the opportunity to think about what I've said. As soon as the meeting ends, I'm going to hand out several graphics: The "schoolhouse" graphic depicts the Comer Process (see Figures 2.2 and 2.3 in the next chapter for English and Spanish versions of this graphic) and the second graphic depicts the six developmental pathways (see Figure 2.1 in the same chapter). I will also make available to all the adults in the school community copies of the book *Six Pathways to Healthy Child Development and Academic Success: The Field Guide to Comer Schools in Action.*

I'd like you to think about what strengths you could bring to a team. At this point, you're supposed to bring this information to your departments and grade-level meetings. Have meetings, discuss it, and be really honest with me. We can have other meetings like this, and you tell me whether it's worth it to do this, or each grade level can write down their concerns and we can meet. I'll take the time after school or whenever to meet with each grade level or each department, and we can have small group discussions as a follow-up to help clarify what this process is about. As I said, if there are some things I can't answer, I'll try to get the answers for you.

Our SDP facilitator explained to me that during the first phase of implementing the Comer Process, we have to study ourselves. The point of the self-assessment is not to assign blame. In fact, the facilitators who will help guide those meetings *won't let us* assign blame!

I am thinking that in five years, we will hold a celebration, like so many other successful schools that use the Comer Process. We will celebrate the successful creation of a school where children learn well because they are developing well. At the celebration, we will laugh as we recall our struggles during the first few years. More important, we will have formed group experiences. We will be a team.

In the meantime, we have a great deal of work ahead of us. After we complete the self-assessment, at our school we will first see if 75 percent of the staff agree to implement the Comer Process. If so, then we will be on our way. Initially, when children are learning new knowledge, they're not sure of themselves. They need a lot of protection, pats on the back, reassurances. Adults, too, need protection while we're learning a new way of working and interacting with one another because we're not quite ready to fly. The Comer Process provides us with a road map: The SDP Implementation Life Cycle. Having a road map for whole-school change gives us the protection that we will need as we embark on change. During the first phases of change, which could take two to three years, we will say to outsiders, "Let us first put our house in order before you come to visit." We don't have to do everything perfectly the first year. However, we know the final destination because we have a road map. Many of the other schools that have gone before us have moved up from being the lowest performing to the highest performing schools in their districts.

REFERENCE

Borman, G. D., Hewes, G. M., Overman, L. T., & Brown, S. (2003). Comprehensive school reform and student achievement: A meta-analysis. *Review of Educational Research, 73*(2), 125-230.

READ MORE ABOUT . . .

To read more about the SDP Implementation Life Cycle, see "The School Development Program Implementation Life Cycle," Chapter 18 in this volume.

2

Essential Understandings of the Yale School Development Program

Yale School Development Program Staff

The comprehensive school reform model known as the Comer Process, or Yale University School Development Program (SDP), was established in 1968 as a collaborative effort between New Haven Public Schools and the Yale Child Study Center, an academic research center dedicated to furthering the well-being of children through a clearer understanding of their psychology and growth. More than three decades of research demonstrate that full implementation of the Comer Process leads to high levels of student achievement and development, and that the Comer Process meets the highest standard of evidence of effectiveness. This chapter provides a brief reference guide to the Comer Process.

SDP AND THE COMER PROCESS

The Yale University School Development Program (SDP) is the forerunner of all modern school reform efforts in the United States. In 1968, a Yale Child Study

Center team that was led by James P. Comer, M.D., intervened in two public schools. The team consisted of a social worker, psychologist, special education teacher, and child psychiatrist. The operating system for schools that emerged during those early years in New Haven schools is today fondly known as the Comer Process.

The Comer Process is an educational change initiative based on the principles of child, adolescent, and adult development. It mobilizes teachers, administrators, parents, and other concerned adults to support students' personal, social, and academic growth. It also helps them make better programmatic and curriculum decisions based on students' needs and on developmental principles. The Comer Process is not a project or add-on, but rather an operating system—a way of managing, organizing, coordinating, and integrating activities. SDP practices considered highly controversial in 1969—whole-school change, school-based management, strong parental involvement in decision making, and teacher study groups—are now common in schools throughout the country.

Over the past three decades, our research and the research of others cited throughout this field guide have consistently found that schools that implement the Comer Process at high levels tend to experience high levels of student achievement and development. In general, schools that demonstrate high levels of implementation are those in which adults

- behave in a way that embodies the Comer Process and mind-set
- demonstrate flexibility and expertise in change management
- relate knowledge of child and youth development to student learning
- make decisions that are in the best interests of children

SIX DEVELOPMENTAL PATHWAYS

Of all the prominent educational reformers, only James P. Comer talks about healthy child development as the keystone to academic achievement and life success. Comer uses a metaphor of six developmental pathways to characterize the lines along which children and adolescents mature—physical, cognitive, psychological, language, social, and ethical (see Figure 2.1). In schools using the Comer Process, far more is expected from the students than just cognitive development.

SDP believes that development is the foundation for all learning:

- Child rearing, child development, and learning are inextricably linked.
- Development starts early and must be a continuous process.
- Children's most meaningful learning occurs through positive and supportive relationships with caring and nurturing adults.
- Parents are children's first teachers.
- All parents, staff, and community members, regardless of social or economic status, have an important contribution to make in improving students' education and their preparation for life; therefore, adults must interact collaboratively and sensitively with one another in order to bring out the best in children.

Figure 2.1 The developmental pathways panel

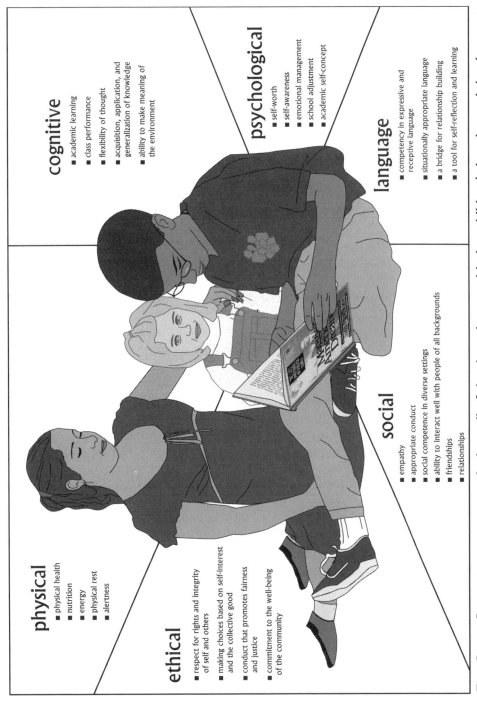

physical
- physical health
- nutrition
- energy
- physical rest
- alertness

cognitive
- academic learning
- class performance
- flexibility of thought
- acquisition, application, and generalization of knowledge
- ability to make meaning of the environment

psychological
- self-worth
- self-awareness
- emotional management
- school adjustment
- academic self-concept

ethical
- respect for rights and integrity of self and others
- making choices based on self-interest and the collective good
- conduct that promotes fairness and justice
- commitment to the well-being of the community

social
- empathy
- appropriate conduct
- social competence in diverse settings
- ability to interact well with people of all backgrounds
- friendships
- relationships

language
- competency in expressive and receptive language
- situationally appropriate language
- a bridge for relationship building
- a tool for self-reflection and learning

The Comer Process promotes growth along all of the six pathways critical to children's learning and development.

SDP is committed to the total development of children and adolescents by helping parents, educators, and policymakers create learning environments that support children's development along the critical pathways. Children who develop well, learn well. Our vision is to help create a just and fair society in which all children have the support for development that will allow them to become positive and successful contributors in family, work, and civic life.

AN OPERATING SYSTEM

The Comer Process provides a structure as well as a process for mobilizing adults to support students' learning and overall development. It is a different way of conceptualizing and working in schools, and it replaces traditional school organization and management with an operating system that works for schools and the students they serve. The schoolhouse graphic in Figures 2.2 and 2.3 displays the nine basic elements of the system.

The following three teams are the hallmark of the Comer Process:

- **School Planning and Management Team:** The SPMT develops a comprehensive school plan; sets academic, social, and community relations goals; and coordinates all school activities, including staff development programs. The team creates critical dialogue around teaching and learning and monitors progress to identify needed adjustments to the school plan as well as opportunities to support the plan. Members of the team include administrators, teachers, support staff, and parents.
- **Student and Staff Support Team:** The SSST promotes desirable social conditions and relationships. It connects all of the school's student services, facilitates the sharing of information and advice, addresses individual student needs, accesses resources outside the school, and develops prevention programs. Membership includes individuals in the school community who possess specialized knowledge, training, or expertise in mental health or child and adolescent development theory and practice.
- **Parent Team:** PT involves parents in the school by developing activities through which the parents can support the school's social and academic programs. Composed of parents, this team also selects representatives to serve on the School Planning and Management Team.

All three teams operate under three Guiding Principles:

- **No-fault:** No-fault maintains the focus on problem solving rather than placing blame. No-fault does not mean no-accountability. It means *everyone* becomes accountable.
- **Consensus:** Through dialogue and understanding, this decision-making process builds consensus about what is good for children and adolescents. All go with what most think will work—understanding that if it doesn't work, other ideas will be tried.
- **Collaboration:** Collaboration encourages the principal and teams to work together. All agree not to "roadblock" the principal, who has legal responsibility; the principal agrees to be responsive to all members.

Figure 2.2 Schoolhouse model of the Comer Process

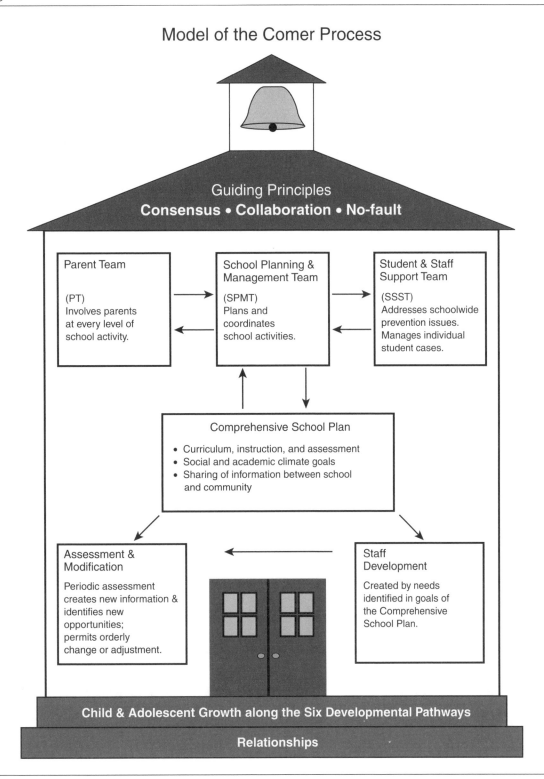

Model of the Comer Process

Guiding Principles
Consensus • Collaboration • No-fault

Parent Team

(PT)
Involves parents at every level of school activity.

School Planning & Management Team

(SPMT)
Plans and coordinates school activities.

Student & Staff Support Team

(SSST)
Addresses schoolwide prevention issues. Manages individual student cases.

Comprehensive School Plan

- Curriculum, instruction, and assessment
- Social and academic climate goals
- Sharing of information between school and community

Assessment & Modification

Periodic assessment creates new information & identifies new opportunities; permits orderly change or adjustment.

Staff Development

Created by needs identified in goals of the Comprehensive School Plan.

Child & Adolescent Growth along the Six Developmental Pathways

Relationships

Figure 2.3 Programa de desarrollo escolar

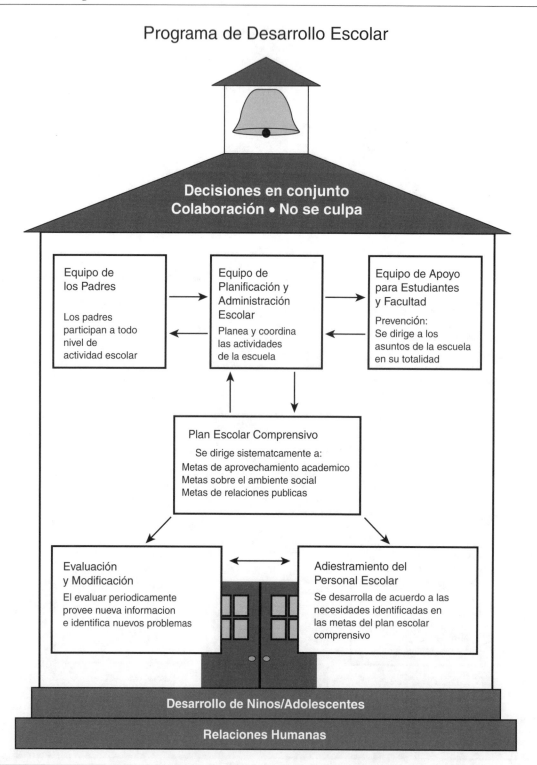

Programa de Desarrollo Escolar

Decisiones en conjunto
Colaboración • No se culpa

Equipo de
los Padres

Los padres
participan a todo
nivel de
actividad escolar

Equipo de
Planificación y
Administración
Escolar

Planea y coordina
las actividades
de la escuela

Equipo de Apoyo
para Estudiantes
y Facultad

Prevención:
Se dirige a los
asuntos de la escuela
en su totalidad

Plan Escolar Comprensivo

Se dirige sistematcamente a:
Metas de aprovechamiento academico
Metas sobre el ambiente social
Metas de relaciones publicas

Evaluación
y Modificación

El evaluar periodicamente
provee nueva informacion
e identifica nuevos problemas

Adiestramiento del
Personal Escolar

Se desarrolla de acuerdo a las
necesidades identificadas en
las metas del plan escolar
comprensivo

Desarrollo de Ninos/Adolescentes

Relaciones Humanas

Central to their work are the following three school operations, which are supervised by the School Planning and Management Team:

- **Comprehensive School Plan:** This planning process includes curriculum, instruction, and assessment, as well as social and academic climate goals based on a developmental understanding of students
- **Staff Development:** Staff development is aligned with the goals of the Comprehensive School Plan; teachers become alert to their own professional development needs and take the lead in designing their own continuing education
- **Assessment & Modification:** This operation provides new information and identifies new opportunities for support, based on the data of the school's population; data are used to modify the school plan as necessary, thus ensuring that the school is continuously improving its operations

A school is permitted to call itself "a fully certified SDP school" only after it has completed the full five-year SDP Life Cycle implementation cycle (see Chapter 18 in *Transforming School Leadership and Management to Support Student Learning and Development*) and the administrators and major teams have met specific behavioral requirements as well as demonstrated excellent knowledge of SDP's approach. Before that time, other labels should be used, for example, "a school in the SDP training program" or "a school in the 1st year (at the 1st stage) of SDP training/implementation."

> For more information on how to become a member of the SDP network, please see our Web site, www.comerprocess.org.

Figure 2.4   School Development Program highlights

- Introduced in 1968 as a process for comprehensive school improvement
- Founded on principles of child development, social relationship theory, and public health
- Nine-element process that fosters positive school climate and creates optimal conditions for teaching and learning
- Not a project or add-on, but a way of managing, organizing, coordinating, and integrating activities
- Provides a strategy for data-driven decision making
- Emphasizes the alignment of curriculum, instruction, and assessment
- Provides schools, districts, and other partners with a framework for communicating and planning to improve conditions for children
- Provides continual support through facilitators and ongoing trainings for adult development as well as child and youth development
- When faithfully and fully implemented, produces extraordinary academic, social, and emotional benefits for the students

THIS FIELD GUIDE

Some members of the school community have a need to approach SDP through a deep understanding of its intellectual foundations. Others need to encounter powerful narratives of how schools improved. Some need to see detailed guidance on what, specifically, they need to do in the classroom. Others need to see how their specialized area fits under SDP's "umbrella." Thus, in our training academies and in this field guide, we provide three types of material:

- narratives that depict SDP in action
- SDP's philosophy
- SDP training materials, including practical exercises

The material in the field guide has been organized in three volumes, as follows:

- *Six Pathways to Healthy Child Development and Academic Success.* The theme of this volume is child and adult development, and the principles that underlie all of our work. To bring out the best in children, we must bring out the best in ourselves.
- *Transforming School Leadership and Management to Support Student Learning and Development.* This volume covers the nine core elements of the Comer Process as they have developed over time.
- *Dynamic Instructional Leadership to Support Student Learning and Development.* This volume continues with Comer Process practices in depth in the classroom, principal leadership, and evaluation of the process. It also describes SDP's approach to systemwide reform that makes the entire district the community of change.

The field guide is a critical resource, but not a replacement for SDP training. Participants in the leadership academies need ways to maintain and review their own experience of the academies once they are back home. They will be responsible for training their school communities in the Comer Process. This field guide will help establish a common language, mind-set, and behavior set within the community.

The take-home message is that *all* members of the school community need to engage in transforming the school—not only the principal or a few key individuals.

RESPONSIBILITIES OF THE SCHOOL COMMUNITY

We believe school communities should

- provide supportive work environments for teachers to maximize their ability to deliver instruction and provide developmental experiences to prepare students for life beyond school
- facilitate positive relationships among parents, students, and school staff to develop the bonds necessary for effective teaching and learning
- be structured to promote collaborative decision making and a culture of inclusion

- promote learning as a lifelong process
- value cultural, linguistic, and ethnic differences to enhance the educational process for all people
- use data from all levels of the system—student, school, and the district—to inform educational policies and practices
- view change as an ongoing process guided by continuous constructive feedback
- design curriculum, instruction, and assessment to align with national, state, and local standards and promote child and community development
- provide administrators with the support they need to lead and manage schools
- promote organizational coherence among school boards, educators, and parents
- provide a sound education with an emphasis on civic responsibility

An education system that fosters child and adolescent development will make it possible to maintain and improve our democratic society.

3

The School Planning and Management Team

The Engine That Drives the School

Miriam McLaughlin, Everol Ennis, and Fred Hernández

Because the faithful implementation of the School Planning and Management Team (SPMT) model is critical to the success of the Comer Process in any school, it is essential that all aspects of the SPMT's purpose, organization, and functioning be well understood by the entire school community. In this chapter, a member of the School Development Program's (SDP) national faculty, an implementation coordinator at the national office of SDP, and a principal describe the SPMT's responsibilities and constituency groups. They map out the first steps in starting an SPMT, and provide rich details about the process of doing the team's work.

The School Planning and Management Team (SPMT) is the lead decision-making and planning body of the school. Team members work to build a community where all members have a voice in the decision-making process. Being the school's central team, the SPMT must set the tone for all other teams and the entire school. Its members must be in accord, and their work should be characterized by a positive climate and the spirit of no-fault.

> The role of the School Planning and Management Team is not to direct people's actions but to make sure people's actions have direction.
>
> —Fred Hernández, principal

SPMT RESPONSIBILITIES

The SPMT has numerous responsibilities, most of which fit into one of the following categories:

- improving curriculum and instruction
- improving students' psychosocial functioning
- improving social relations among adults, among students, and between adults and students
- establishing policy guidelines for school programs
- responding to school concerns either directly or by delegating the response to a subcommittee that will report back to appropriate persons and groups
- carrying out systematic school planning
- creating effective programs for staff development, parent training, academics, social climate, and public relations
- planning an annual school calendar that integrates social, academic, and staff development functions
- monitoring and evaluating the Comprehensive School Plan and all school programs
- promoting effective resource utilization, coordination, and program implementation

The SPMT is responsible for coordinating and aligning the activities of the school based on the Comprehensive School Plan to ensure consistency and the equitable distribution of resources. The team should demonstrate a strong academic focus in planning, based on child and adolescent development principles and a child-development-centered agenda. Figure 3.1 shows how these responsibilities are related to the team's developmental stages.

Figure 3.1 Developmental stages of a School Planning and Management Team

Stage	Major Theme	Dependent On
One	• Inclusion • Process orientation • Engagement	• Whole-school community awareness • Open leadership style • Creation of initial successes
Two	• Coordination and alignment of all school activities • Joint problem solving • Greater authority sharing • Initiation of child-centered planning	• School community buy-in • Skills in group interaction • Collaborative leadership style • Skills in discerning important patterns from data • User-friendly data • Knowledge of developmental pathways
Three	• Creation of a child-centered agenda • Reflection on teaching and learning	• Knowing students well across developmental pathways • Strong global Student and Staff Support Team • Strong parent views • Strong instructional leadership

Figure 3.2 Template depicting constituency groups

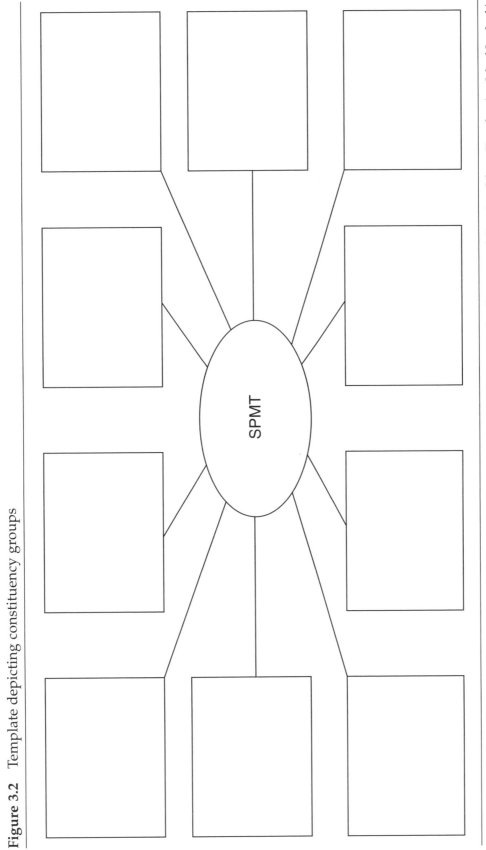

CONSTITUENCY GROUPS

To keep the business of the school achievable, the SPMT must be manageable and inclusive of those members who have a stake in the students' success. The SPMT should not be so large that meetings are difficult to run and not so small that certain groups of the school community are left out. In addition, the SPMT should have members who are dedicated to the school's mission and vision and do not divert or subvert the SPMT with hidden personal agendas. The SPMT is made up of representatives of all parts of the school community. *This inclusiveness is what makes the SPMT different from the management teams found in most schools.* Another distinction is that the SPMT uses the six developmental pathways as a framework for developing programs and activities for students. Through the SPMT, administrators, parents, teachers, and other professionals, such as subject specialists and health and guidance staff, noninstructional staff, members of the community, and in some cases, students, play significant roles in the management of the school (see Figure 3.2 for a template of how to graphically depict constituency groups). Figure 3.3 lists the constituency groups that are the irreducible core of any SPMT.

Administrators

Another characteristic of the SPMT that differs from traditional management teams is the sharing of leadership. In all schools, principals hold leadership and decision-making roles. When they are working with an SPMT, their challenge is to ensure that the school meets all requirements and mandates of the district and state offices, while they share the leadership of the school and collaborate with other members of the SPMT. Despite being a key team member, a principal should not serve as chair of the SPMT. It does not help to foster the notion of collaboration or shared leadership if the leader of the building is also the leader of the meeting of the lead team in the building. The principal works with the chairperson of the SPMT

Figure 3.3   Checklist of SPMT constituency groups

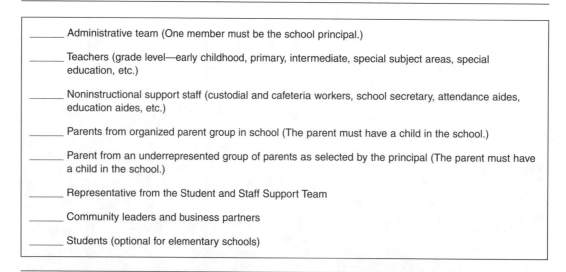

_____ Administrative team (One member must be the school principal.)

_____ Teachers (grade level—early childhood, primary, intermediate, special subject areas, special education, etc.)

_____ Noninstructional support staff (custodial and cafeteria workers, school secretary, attendance aides, education aides, etc.)

_____ Parents from organized parent group in school (The parent must have a child in the school.)

_____ Parent from an underrepresented group of parents as selected by the principal (The parent must have a child in the school.)

_____ Representative from the Student and Staff Support Team

_____ Community leaders and business partners

_____ Students (optional for elementary schools)

and the Comer facilitator to build the agenda before each meeting. Most effective administrators arrange to have some time on the agenda allotted to their business; the rest of the time, their role is to be an involved participant on the team. (It can be very frustrating to other team members when the SPMT meeting serves as the principal's meeting for the entire time allotted. If this occurs, a postmeeting debriefing session to assess how the SPMT performed is one means of addressing the team process.)

Instructional Staff

All instructional staff should have representation on the SPMT. Delegates may come from grade-level teams, special subject area teams, and subcommittees. Thus, they can bring their concerns and needs from the smaller group to the larger team and have a voice in the management of the school. In return, they are expected to bring the larger management issues that are being raised back to their constituent group or team. This linkage is most effective when the representatives (1) have regular contact with the teachers at their grade-level or other meetings, (2) report regularly on the discussions and considerations taking place in the SPMT, and (3) are efficient about bringing concerns, needs, and ideas of the teachers to the SPMT meetings—exclusive of personal issues. Making minutes of the SPMT meetings available in a timely manner is also important in assuring that teachers feel they have a voice in the management of the school. If the school does not have the resources to make minutes available to everyone, a copy of minutes can be placed in a centrally located area (e.g., the main office). It is important that this copy be easily accessible to all members of the school community.

Noninstructional Staff

As indicated above, all members of the school community must be involved in the decision making in the school. Perhaps one of the most important constituency groups, and one often overlooked, is the noninstructional support staff. Custodians, cafeteria workers, clerical, and support staff have a unique view of the school and the students and can be valuable contributors to the management team. To ensure their representation, it is often necessary to form a noninstructional staff subcommittee that has established meeting times and that chooses a representative to the SPMT. The school-based facilitator is present at the noninstructional staff subcommittee meetings, as his or her schedule permits, to lend support. Consideration must be given to the often diverse work schedules of this group and their availability for meetings.

Parents

The Parent Team (PT), PTA/PTO, and similar parent groups are usually accustomed to school involvement, and it is not difficult to get representation on the SPMT from these groups. These parent organizations play an important role in the life of the school. They are frequently already collaborating on the school calendar, and they often have access to funds that can support SPMT projects. However, bake sales and fund raising are not enough. Parents on the SPMT must be positioned to help the school community move forward in meeting its social and academic goals for the students. Their delegate to the SPMT is an important link to many of the school's families.

Much more challenging is reaching parents from underrepresented groups in the school community. These parents are more likely to be uncomfortable about being involved in the business of the school. They may have had unpleasant experiences in school themselves or have limited knowledge of the education process. One way schools are successful in involving the uninvolved parents is to identify a parent liaison who is representative of a particular socioeconomic or ethnic group. This individual is an employee of the school who is accessible to parents, often meeting with them in their homes. Through these contacts, parents are identified who are able and willing to attend SPMT meetings. Also, administrators and teachers can work together to identify and seek out parents they think would be willing to serve. Frequently, schools will start by implementing a PT. A parent representative is then selected from that team to serve on the SPMT.

> The professional community tends to overlook the tremendous resource parents can be.
>
> —Fred Hernández, principal

Student and Staff Support Team

The Student and Staff Support Team (SSST) also provides leadership in the Comer Process. This team deals with the needs of individual students and works to identify global school issues or trends. The job of the SSST is to intervene for the well-being of students and the well-being of the school. Its representative brings to the SPMT problems the SSST has identified and its recommendations for prevention.

Community Partners

Many schools are fortunate to have community partners. These are businesses, universities, and organizations (civic, private, religious, etc.) that take an active interest in the life of the school. They are sometimes financial contributors, and often encourage their employees to serve as mentors for students who need extra help or support. These partners may offer free merchandise, goods, or services for school events. In addition, a university department that is collaborating with the school may provide students and teaching staff. Schools that have such partnerships should include representatives from these organizations on the SPMT. They are important contacts to the community and its resources. It is important that the best interests of children remain the overriding reason for participation.

Students

Student participation on the SPMT is optional for elementary schools. Some SPMTs invite elementary school students to participate in discussions on specific topics or be part of planning for special events. When student councils or student government organizations (SGOs) are in place in an elementary school, they should be informed of the role of the SPMT and of any opportunities SGO members may have to participate in meetings. Middle and high school students, however, should routinely be involved to some degree on the SPMT. Student government should be kept informed of the activities of the SPMT, even when meeting times and school activities prohibit students' regular attendance at SPMT meetings. Bear in mind that an SGO is only one

> We encourage all schools to establish a Comer Kids' Council. The purpose of the Comer Kids' Council is to promote leadership among the students in the school. Schools can turn their current student government associations into Comer Kids' Councils in the same way that schools may modify their preexisting leadership teams under the guidance of the Comer Process. (See "Proud to Be a Comer Kid," in Chapter 5 of *Six Pathways to Healthy Child Development and Academic Success: The Field Guide to Comer Schools in Action* in this series.)

means of selecting a student representative to the SPMT. There may be other students who are qualified to serve and are not members of an SGO. The goal is to ensure a link between the SPMT and the student body.

FIRST STEPS IN STARTING AN SPMT

How does a school ensure that everyone in the school community is represented on the SPMT? Compare a list of potential constituency groups with a current SPMT membership list. Identify the SPMT member who represents each individual and group. Publicize that information to ensure that all members of the school community know who represents them. Please point out that anyone from the school community is welcome to attend an SPMT meeting, as it is a public forum. However, if visitors want to present issues, they must ask to be put on the agenda through their constituent group. If their constituent group is in agreement that the issue is an appropriate use of SPMT meeting time, then that issue is brought by their SPMT representative. Figure 3.4 offers an exercise through which SPMTs can assess whether they are appropriately inclusive.

The first steps an SPMT should take include the following:

1. Determine who will serve on the team and for how long.

2. Decide on meeting dates and times for the year. Place these dates on your master calendar.

3. Know each other. Ongoing team building reinforces relationships and encourages best instructional practices.

4. Know your students. Create a large visual chart including the following:
   neighborhood demographics
   student demographics
   test data
   attendance data
   referral data
   developmental data
   climate data
   other information about students

5. Know what you already do. Create a large visual chart that includes the following:
   all current teams
   all current subcommittees
   all current programs
   all instructional initiatives

6. Assess your school program. Identify
   current strengths
   current weaknesses
   what can be cut back or eliminated (through a decision-making process based on consensus)
   the short-term and long-term priorities, based on your Comprehensive School Plan

Figure 3.4 An example of how a school allocated SPMT membership

Staff Allocation	SPMT Membership
1 principal	principal
1 assistant principal	assistant principal
2 secretaries	librarian
1 nurse	Comer facilitator
1 librarian	PTA president
6 cafeteria workers	2 first-grade teachers
4 custodial engineers	1 third-grade teacher
1 guidance counselor	special education teacher
1 technology specialist	reading specialist
1 Comer facilitator	instructional specialist
1 parent facilitator	

Teachers
  5 kindergarten
  5 first
  5 second
  5 third
  3 fourth
  3 fifth
  1 reading specialist
  1 instructional specialist
  2 special education

Instructional Aides
  5 kindergarten
  5 first

Questions

- Does this school's SPMT include representation from all the key stakeholders in the building?
- Who is missing?
- Are any groups overrepresented?
- How should SPMT members be selected?
- How long should SPMT members serve?

GETTING TO KNOW EACH OTHER, THE STUDENTS, AND THE COMMUNITY

How well do members of your SPMT know each other? Team members must have relationships with one another in order to work productively as a team. Team building is an important first step for an SPMT. Going on a retreat together is one of the most effective ways to promote relationships. However, team building should also be part of every agenda. It takes just a few minutes at the beginning of the meeting for people to check in with one another and reconnect.

To accomplish the tasks of the SPMT, including the development of the Comprehensive School Plan, members must know the students who are attending the school and the communities the school serves. In addition, SPMT members will want to look at what is already in place in the school in terms of current teams, programs, and instructional initiatives. This information will help the team identify strengths and gaps and will point the way to priorities for the school year.

STRUCTURING THE MEETINGS

From the outset, it is important to have shared agreements about procedures, to stay on task, and to be clear about the expected attendance and tenure of the team members.

Shared Agreements

Ask the team to work together to build a list of specific behaviors they can commit to that will help the team to work effectively. For example, starting and ending on time is important to all members of the team. That means team members will take responsibility for getting to the meetings on time and will stick to the agenda during discussions. Write shared agreements about these behaviors on chart paper (or something even more permanent) and post them on the wall during every meeting.

Staying on Task

Time, topics, tasks, and roles of members are all important considerations when holding a meeting. Nothing is more frustrating to team members than unstructured meetings that do not accomplish what was intended, go on indefinitely, and pull team members in at the last minute to perform tasks for which they are unprepared. The end result of such meetings is an unwillingness on the part of staff, parents, and community members to serve on teams. We encourage the chair or facilitator to periodically check in with team members to ensure that the meeting is proceeding as planned.

Tenure on the Team

The SPMT seeks volunteers or nominates people for specific roles on the team. These individuals usually keep their roles for at least two years, with half the team rotating off each year. If SPMT members serve only one-year terms, that puts the SPMT in the position of "starting from scratch" each school year. Ideally, team members should have three-year terms, so that only one-third of the team would change each year. This approach allows the SPMT to have continuity, while giving others in the school community opportunities to serve in leadership roles. Anything longer than three years could lead to burn-out or resentment by other staff members. In addition, if new staff members perceive the SPMT as the team that "doesn't like to share the leadership responsibilities," they may become discouraged about trying to become members.

The Agenda

The agenda for the SPMT is developed jointly by the chairperson, the Comer facilitator, and the principal a week before the meeting, allowing ample time for members to propose any corrections or additions. All members of the SPMT can contribute agenda items during this time, as long as the issues are ones that have emerged from discussions in the constituent groups represented on the SPMT. An agenda item should never come from an individual, with the exception of a school community visitor who wishes to address the SPMT during the meeting. (The visitor's issues should be screened to determine if the SPMT should address the issue.) For example, an SPMT agenda item pertaining to the Parent Team should come from the parents on that team and not solely from the Parent Team representative on the SPMT. To make sure that the agenda items are appropriate, they should be discussed by committees and teams before they are submitted to the SPMT.

Contributors to the agenda are asked about the amount of time needed during the meeting to address their item, and time is assigned. The assigned amount of time for each agenda item should fit within the allotted time for the meeting. Agenda items that come in late or will extend the meeting over its allotted time should be moved to the next meeting. If urgent business arises, the agenda should be revisited and less urgent items moved to the next meeting's agenda. Adherence to the time allotted is critical to the success of the SPMT. The meetings often take place after school, and team members have personal responsibilities to tend to after the meeting. If the meeting runs for an unpredictable length of time, team members will leave or become less focused on business. Time is monitored by the timekeeper, who pays close attention to the times assigned to each agenda topic. If the members wish to continue a discussion beyond the time allotted, they can negotiate for additional minutes with the timekeeper and the rest of the SPMT using consensus decision making. Figure 3.5 offers a sample format that can be used for an SPMT agenda and for meeting minutes.

Agenda Topics

The work of the SPMT is guided by the goals of the Comprehensive School Plan. At least 75 percent of the meeting should focus on the Comprehensive School Plan. The team focuses on the academic and developmental needs of students, the professional growth and staff development needs of teachers, and the social climate of the school. Curriculum is a very important topic for the team to consider. It is critical that the team have comprehensive data regarding student performance in all subject areas to guide decision making. For example, if the team is considering a reading program for the primary grades, it should have (at a minimum) data on reading performance for students in those grades and at the higher grade levels.

> Appropriate discussion (for the SPMT) obviously has to do with curriculum items . . . and sharing data. For example, the perception on the fourth-grade English language arts test is that whatever the results are, the fourth-grade teachers are responsible for that. But looking at fourth-grade data and not looking at the data on kindergarten leading up to fourth (not seeing the whole picture) is not appropriate.
>
> —Fred Hernández, principal

The activities of the school are coordinated by the SPMT with input from all other teams and subcommittees. It is important that team members understand what is appropriate and what is inappropriate to discuss at team meetings. Discussion of inappropriate topics can pull an SPMT from its purpose. The following issues are appropriate for discussion at an SPMT meeting:

- agenda items
- instruction and curriculum
- school social events
- public relations
- school climate and school environment

Issues concerning just a few members of the school community, individual students or their families, personnel issues, and complaints are not the business of the SPMT. Those issues are handled by administrators and other appropriate school personnel.

In addition, subcommittees may be assigned to handle certain tasks that arise during an SPMT meeting. Among the tasks that are referred to subcommittees are suggested policies or programs that require research before a decision can be made, as well as events that require planning.

> Inappropriate [discussion on the SPMT] would be blaming teachers, blaming parents, blaming the administration—the blame game.
>
> —Fred Hernández, principal

PROCESS: THE GUIDING PRINCIPLES

With the SPMT, as with the entire SDP, how the work is accomplished is as important as the tasks themselves. In fact, the work of the SPMT is only as effective as the process used to accomplish tasks. The guiding principles of consensus, collaboration, and no-fault are the foundation of all SDP interactions.

ALL DECISIONS MADE IN THE BEST INTERESTS OF CHILDREN

The SPMT is responsible for maintaining the school's focus on the needs of children. Agenda items, discussions, and decisions should all be guided by the question, "What is best for children?" The most effective way for the SPMT to gain this perspective is to ensure that all members of the school community are well-versed in the knowledge of the six developmental pathways that are critical to children's growth and academic learning.

TROUBLESHOOTING: HOW DOES THE SPMT DECIDE . . .

. . . When to Meet?

Keep in mind that you are involving a good number of school staff as well as parents and community members in the meetings. Most management teams find that

Figure 3.5   Sample form for SPMT meeting minutes

Date:			
Team Members Attending:			
Chair: Facilitator: Recorder: Timekeeper: Other:			

Agenda Item	Discussion/Decision	Person(s) Responsible	Follow-up Dates
1.			
2.			
3.			
4.			
5.			

6.			
7.			
8.			
9.			
10.			

Next Team Meeting Date:	**Location:**
Time:	**Invited Guests:**
Agenda Items:	

NOTES, IMPORTANT DATES, EVENTS, REMINDERS:

after-school meetings work best. Some schools' SPMTs meet in the evening or in the morning before the start of the school day to ensure that parents will be able to attend. Alternating meeting times can also increase the opportunities for parents and community members to attend. Meeting times should be determined by consensus of the team members. However, flexibility is important. The team should meet at least two times per month.

. . . How to Deal With a Principal Who Dominates the Meetings?

It is not unusual for principals to have difficulty sharing leadership. To help guide administrators, teams can review the roles at every meeting and remind administrators of their role as group members.

Also, the chairpersons and facilitators can work with administrators ahead of time to identify those agenda items on which it is appropriate for them to lead. The name of each person speaking about an agenda item can be identified and recorded ahead of time. It is the facilitator's responsibility to keep any team member from dominating discussions. This approach requires that team members trust their administrators and vice versa. If nothing else works during the public forum, private discussion about the impact of the administrator's behavior on the rest of the team may be useful. This discussion is probably best coming from a fellow team member who has a good relationship with the administrator.

> The purpose of the team is about altering power relationships. It's not about just the symbolic. If you only address the symbolic, business proceeds as usual. You have representation, but then you have the same problems within the team that you have in the regular school day. The team can start altering those relationships. So that is why it is important that the instructional leader—the principal—takes a risk and has the courage to allow the team to make the decisions.
>
> —Fred Hernández, principal

. . . How to Deal With Resistance?

There is always some resistance in the beginning. Usually, the resistance stems from negative past experiences, which cause people to be reluctant to change. Most people find change uncomfortable, even when they know the old ways are not working. It is important to stress that the SPMT will not be taking on additional work, but rather learning more effective and efficient ways of working. To counteract resistance, the majority of the SPMT must support and participate in the new methods and attitudes of the Comer Process. In a sense, the SPMT will set the tone of acceptance for the whole school community. Furthermore, it is critical that the rest of the SPMT members listen to the resistant members. These individuals may or may not have something valid or positive to contribute. However, if they don't feel that the rest of the team is genuinely listening, the resistant members will be disinterested for the remainder of their term and may end up sabotaging or subverting the team's efforts.

> You are going to have a subculture that will be resistant. But over time the SDP should become the dominant culture—the way you do business.
>
> —Fred Hernández, principal

. . . What We Can and Can't Do as a Team?

Some SPMTs buy into the notion of shared leadership and the guiding principles so much that they operate outside of their responsibilities and authority. This can create problems. There are some clearly defined issues that should involve only the administrator. The sooner these issues are clarified, the less conflict there will be and the better the relationship will develop between the team and administrator. Personnel issues, for example, are between the principal and the staff member with the problem. Financial issues such as salaries also come under the category of privileged information. There are decisions that only the principal can make, and often those come as a result of dictates from the school system's central office.

> The central office hires the principal, but the SPMT should be part of the process. The hope is that the SDP is systemically part of the school culture, and as principals come and go the team is still there. It becomes so engraved in the culture of the building that it stays in place whatever the changes.
>
> —Fred Hernández, principal

On the other hand, the SPMT can, and should, serve on interview committees, especially when a new administrator is being hired. After all, the new principal's knowledge about and receptivity to SDP will have a direct impact on the continued success of the program. The SPMT and the new administrator should have this discussion at the first possible opportunity to avoid misunderstandings later on.

READ MORE ABOUT . . .

For a full discussion of team building, see "Teaming and Team Building," Chapter 10 in *Six Pathways to Healthy Child Development and Academic Success: The Field Guide to Comer Schools in Action* in this series.

For a full discussion of the principles, see "Three Guiding Principles for Interactions on Teams," Chapter 14 in *Six Pathways to Healthy Child Development and Academic Success: The Field Guide to Comer Schools in Action* in this series.

For a full discussion of SPMT subcommittees, see "School Planning and Management Team (SPMT) Subcommittees," Chapter 7 in this volume.

4

Identifying the Problem You Are Trying to Solve With the Comer Process

SuAnne Lawrence, Michelle Adler Morrison, Michael Ben-Avie, Jonathon H. Gillette, and Gretchen Myhre

We have found through our work with school communities that it is useful to ask, "What problem are you trying to solve with the Comer Process?" Some schools answer, "curriculum" or "instruction." Others answer, "development" or "relationships." Depending on their answer, School Development Program (SDP) facilitators design tailor-made interventions. Using questions to identify critical issues, and a flow chart, a nest, and a rainbow as diagrams of possible problem-solving processes, the authors demonstrate how using visual metaphors can help clarify communications in schools.

ORGANIZING AND MANAGING CRITICAL ISSUES

When issues are defined, organized, and managed effectively, they provide a global picture of what's happening in the school. Once you define and organize these issues, you can begin to gather meaningful data about them. The more thoroughly you analyze those data, the clearer the picture will become.

Staff Activity 4.1: Identifying Critical Issues

Thinking about your own school, identify critical issues and sort them into the categories listed below.

Child Development or Developmental Understanding

- _____
- _____
- _____

Relationships

- _____
- _____
- _____

Instruction

- _____
- _____
- _____

Curriculum

- _____
- _____
- _____

Now reflect about those critical issues:

What patterns seem to emerge?

Do some issues seem to take priority?

Which issues need further clarification before they can be addressed?

SOURCE: Valerie Maholmes, Yale School Development Program.

The School Development Program (SDP) has made contributions in a number of areas related to the problems schools want to solve: parent involvement, school climate, coordinated supportive services, and data-driven, site-based planning. SDP defines teaching and learning broadly, which includes not only curriculum and instruction but also relationships and student development. Still, what distinguishes the SDP as a comprehensive school reform model is that it provides a clear, systematic process that integrates the complex world of daily schooling. The key to that work is a planning process that is student focused and takes into account child development.

CHILD DEVELOPMENT: THE STUDENT-FOCUSED PLANNING PROCESS AS A FLOW CHART by Jonathon H. Gillette

Imagine the beginning of any day in any school. There is high energy as students pour in and find their way to their classrooms. The bell rings, everyone settles down, and in each classroom a teacher looks out at 20 to 30 students, all with their hopes, fears, and expectations. The task is enormous: to meet students where they are and move them toward being able to meet world-class standards. This requires a deep understanding of each student, effective teaching and learning, and a supportive context.

The SDP takes the position that understanding a student well is rooted in knowledge of child and adolescent development. In essence, cognitive growth is a developmental strength that is interconnected with other developmental strengths. The SDP identifies six developmental pathways: physical, cognitive, psychological, language, social, and ethical. Even in settings with world-class curricula, instruction can flounder when educators assume that a student already has a developmental capacity that has not yet emerged or been developed. While this assumption is true of traditional instruction, it is especially true of new, more experiential and cooperative learning techniques.

Developmental strengths are vital if students are to work well together, make sound judgments, and use their considerable natural curiosity to pursue increasingly complex questions. Understanding a student well also requires a positive relationship between the teacher and student, one that can bridge gender, racial, ethnic, and class differences. Teachers must be able to move from their initial reactions and assumptions about a child to a dialogue that creates enough trust for the child to show who he is and what he can do. I will never forget watching a kindergarten child who had learned to suppress all of his natural curiosity as a means of surviving in his neighborhood. Because the child was passive and extremely withdrawn, the teacher saw that her first task was to create a strong bond with him so that he would simply dare to leave his seat.

SDP defines teaching and learning more broadly than other school reform groups. We agree that curriculum and instruction are at the core of the work, and at the same time we assert and demonstrate that relationships and students' development need to be taken into account (see Figure 4.1). These four components are always interacting in classrooms. Collectively, they hold the key to effective practice. Each is necessary but not always sufficient. I have visited classrooms with warm relationships and ineffective instruction. I have seen sophisticated instruction pass over the heads of students whose thoughts were elsewhere.

Figure 4.1   Student-focused planning process

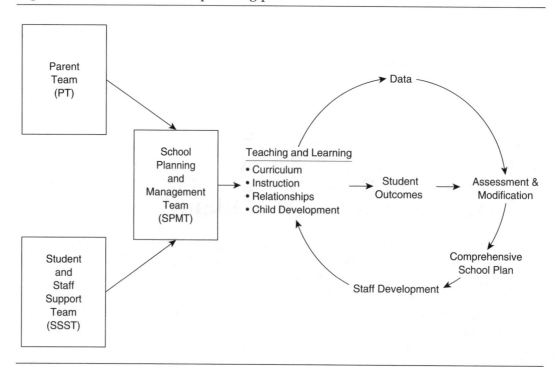

Most important, all teachers experience all four elements of teaching and learning. The usual focus on curriculum and instruction alone does not allow them to diagnose and understand their learning environments fully. I have observed dialogues among teachers in which this extended definition of teaching and learning has led them to new types of problem solving based on strengthening a developmental skill, which, in turn, has led to greater cognitive growth.

The ability to attend to both relationships and development is enhanced when SDP structures are in place. The School Planning and Management Team (SPMT), for example, provides a supportive context for effective planning that integrates many classrooms and grade levels. The SPMT also aligns adults—professionals and parents alike—with a shared vision. Equally important, the SDP allows people to share knowledge and expertise. Parents and guardians have important general cultural knowledge and specific knowledge about their children, as well as individual skills and qualities of being that can enhance the SDP process. Members of the Student and Staff Support Team (SSST) have developmental expertise and often the best overall data on patterns of student behavior. The SDP provides teachers with critical partners as they face the complex set of choices that confront them every day in their classrooms.

All of this is tied together by a planning process that is based on knowledge of child and adolescent development. As Figure 4.1 shows, the SDP planning process goes well beyond simply increasing activity in areas already under way. SDP provides a process for taking a comprehensive look at all of the activities in a school, including parent activities, the work of the SSST, and after-school programs. Many schools have layered developmental programs taking place outside classrooms with no way of connecting them where they may be needed most—within classrooms. Mentoring programs, conflict resolution programs, chess clubs, and drill teams all address a child's overall development.

This planning process uses a wide variety of student data to assess a child's overall development. This process also raises basic questions about how teaching and learning are organized:

- Is our instruction aligned with students' developmental strengths?
- Is our curriculum aligned?
- Are students able to relate culturally to the content presented?
- Does our staff have the skills needed to move our students toward performing at a world-class level?
- Do our staff development efforts help to move the whole school forward?
- In short, if we really know our students, are we ready to do what is needed?

These broader questions allow schools to look at their work more reflectively, to see how each adult contributes, and to design interventions that build a caring and effective learning community.

The morning bell rings, students enter classrooms, and take their seats. The SDP teacher notes that they are acting as a more coherent group, the result of some developmental activities planned by the grade-level planning group and carried out by the gym teacher. Earlier, he ran into a parent in the front hall and heard about a cultural festival that was held on Saturday. Later this morning he is expecting a visit from another teacher, who will share some techniques for effective instruction with math manipulatives. While the day is certainly going to be busy, there is a feeling of connectedness that makes it seem manageable. There is a strong sense that all the adults working together can make a difference so that their students will be ready for adult life.

NEW VISUAL METAPHORS by SuAnne Lawrence, Michelle Adler Morrison, Michael Ben-Avie, and Gretchen Myhre

The diagrams we draw to describe our ideas are visual metaphors and also learning tools to help others understand (1) our view of the task, (2) the task's value in fulfilling the Comprehensive School Plan, and (3) the action steps we think are necessary to accomplish the task. In the previous section, Figure 4.1 shows the student-focused planning process as a flowchart. The diagram is useful because it clearly depicts planning as an ongoing process in SDP schools. Of course, no single diagram could possibly capture a complex human process. In the conversations that follow, the authors use the images of a flow chart, a nest, and a rainbow to demonstrate how creating a variety of diagrams, with the four key terms ordered in different ways, helps clarify communications in schools.

PROMOTING POSITIVE STUDENT OUTCOMES: THE STUDENT-FOCUSED PLANNING PROCESS AS A NEST

SuANNE LAWRENCE: I think you get at developmental issues through curriculum, instruction, and strategies. There are all kinds of curricular activities—literature, social studies, science, and math—that relate to the various developmental pathways. These curricular activities enhance children's understanding and experience with those pathways. Then there are also instructional strategies that a teacher can use to help foster development (e.g., cooperative learning strategies, when used well, can promote development in the social, psychological, and ethical pathways). The various classroom management strategies a teacher uses can promote and, perhaps more important, inhibit development. Strategies that use a student's strengths to correct inappropriate behavior are particularly effective. How teachers act is also important. When you watch exemplary teachers, they use themselves to promote self-esteem, respect and honesty, relationships, decision making, cognitive capacities, and ways of communicating just in how they talk to students and interact with them. Thus, there are four ways: curricular activities, instructional strategies, classroom management strategies, and a way of being with students that is based on an understanding of development and relationships. Teachers have to reach students through all these ways. I think that is what is really important for teachers to understand. We are always in the process of developing children in every interaction we have with them. All of these pathways overlap and interact with one another, just as the curriculum, instruction, classroom management strategies, and use of self overlap and interact with each other. When we are first learning about a student-focused approach, it is easy to treat each of the pathways as a separate entity and try to address each individually.

MICHAEL BEN-AVIE: And what would you suggest?

SuANNE LAWRENCE: I think you have to read about a student-focused approach, receive in-service trainings about it, and equally as important, it has to be modeled for you. You have to see other people do it; you have to be given coaching and feedback while you're doing it.

MICHAEL BEN-AVIE: Let's consider for a moment the usefulness of a diagram as a learning tool (see Figure 4.2). What would you want to convey with a diagram?

Figure 4.2 Promoting positive student outcomes

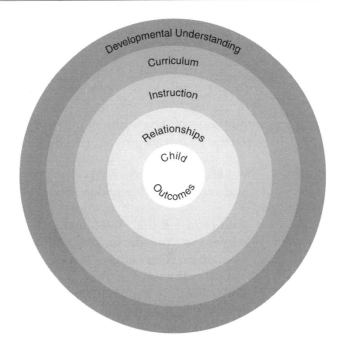

What problem are you trying to solve with the Comer Process?

SuANNE LAWRENCE: I would talk about how we go about trying to change teaching and learning to promote more positive child outcomes.

MICHAEL BEN-AVIE: In the diagram, you would put "child outcomes" in the center.

SuANNE LAWRENCE: Yes, in the center. That's the target. And that's how we change teaching and learning: It is about how the school understands the needs of the students, what the mandates of the district are, the school's resources, and how the school community organizes itself to promote positive student outcomes. For example, if the problem in the building is that there's not enough parent involvement, then that's what the building has to work on.

MICHAEL BEN-AVIE: Well, I would put that under "developmental understanding." Parent involvement is part of children's development—what children need in order to develop well.

MICHELLE ADLER: "Developmental understanding" should be the outer circle. If you have a strong developmental understanding, it will influence how you deliver the curriculum and your instructional strategies.

SuANNE LAWRENCE: I think that on the diagram "instruction" and "relationships" have to be right next to child outcomes. Let's imagine "child outcomes" in the center. Your understanding of development influences how you deliver the curriculum and how you relate to the students.

MICHELLE ADLER: Relationships either have to be right next to child outcomes or right outside instruction.

SuANNE LAWRENCE: Right. So I think "relationships" go next to child outcomes. So your developmental understanding supports everything. Curriculum informs instruction. Instruction supports the relationships, and relationships support the child. Because I'm picturing it like a bowl. In my mind it's not flat. It's almost spherical. I think a better way of understanding the diagram is "circles nesting within one another." Nesting protects and holds the child. If you have a strong developmental understanding, it's going to support curriculum that's going to support instruction and relationships.

TEACHING AND LEARNING: THE STUDENT-FOCUSED PLANNING PROCESS AS A RAINBOW

MICHAEL BEN-AVIE: I could also argue that here's the child in the center and what's closest to the child? "Relationships." Relationships are formed by an understanding of development. The farthest from the child is actually the curriculum because that doesn't come from within the classroom; it comes from the school district or state mandates and so forth. So in terms of proximal influences and how far things are from the child, there are outside influences that are impacting the relationships within the classroom.

MICHELLE ADLER: Instruction directly relates to the child. "Curriculum" may be farther out, but "instruction" has to be connected to "relationships."

SuANNE LAWRENCE: The effectiveness of Figure 4.3 is the extent to which it will help school communities think through what problem they are trying to solve with the Comer Process.

Figure 4.3   What problem are you trying to solve with the Comer Process?

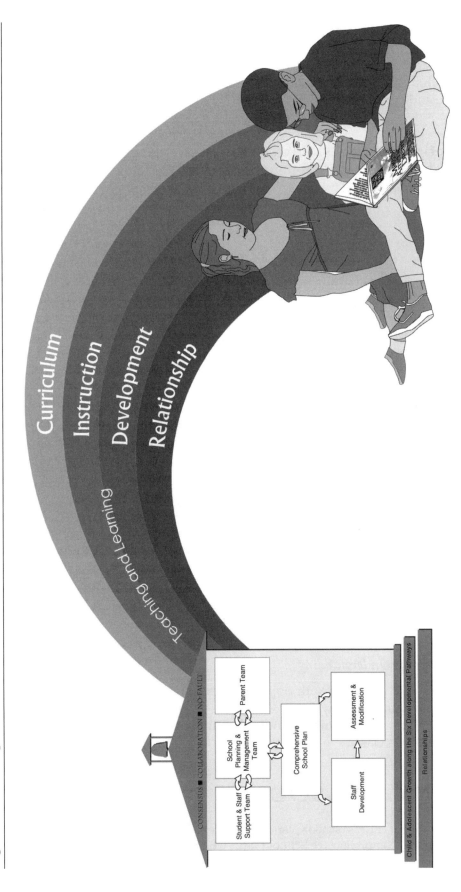

DEFINING THE PROBLEM

One way to start defining the problem that you want the Comer Process to solve is to ask questions about the school's understanding of development, relationships, curriculum, and instruction.

Staff Activity 4.2: Asking Essential Questions

SDP's Valerie Maholmes and Jan Stocklinski encourage school communities to ask themselves the following questions:

Curriculum

- Is the printed curriculum being taught?
- Are there connections made from the curriculum to the lives of the students?
- Are connections made between different areas of the curriculum?
- Are the core curriculum content standards built into each lesson and unit?
- Is the curriculum aligned with local, state, and national assessments?

Instruction

- How many different instructional strategies are used on a regular basis?
- Are opportunities provided for students to learn in small groups?
- What are the specific learning activities that students are expected to do?

Relationships

- Is there evidence that the students engage in ongoing team building activities?
- Is there evidence of positive and caring relationships among the students and between the students and staff members?
- Are visitors welcome in the classroom?
- Do the students interact with one another according to the guiding principles of no-fault, consensus, and collaboration?

Developmental Understanding

- Are students provided with opportunities to be supported along each of the developmental pathways?
- How well do staff members know the students beyond what they reveal of themselves in class?

READ MORE ABOUT . . .

To read more about SDP's school-planning process based on child development, see "Designing the Comprehensive School Plan," Chapter 6 in this volume.

To read more about SDP's approach to classroom practices, see "Comer-in-the-Classroom," Chapter 6 in *Dynamic Instructional Leadership to Support Student Learning and Development: The Field Guide to Comer Schools in Action* in this series.

To read more about SDP's approach to the alignment of curriculum, instruction, and assessment, see "Curriculum Structure and Teacher Planning," Chapter 5 in *Dynamic Instructional Leadership to Support Student Learning and Development: The Field Guide to Comer Schools in Action* in this series.

5

All Decisions
Must Be Made in
the Best Interests
of Children

SDP's Most Important Standard

**Michael Ben-Avie, Trudy Raschkind Steinfeld,
and James P. Comer**

The statement that "all decisions must be made in the best interests of children" literally occupies the center of the table at all SDP team meetings. It has a fascinating history and leads to a wide range of effects. It also presupposes that team members actually can arrive at decisions and act to carry them out. This commentary presents the background of the central tenet of the Comer Process and offers an in-depth look at the substructure of the decision-making process.

THE BEST-INTERESTS
STANDARD AND SDP

How to make decisions in the best interests of the child was "in the air" at the Yale Child Study Center when the School Development Program (SDP) was in its formative period. In 1968, Albert J. Solnit, Sterling Professor of Pediatrics and Psychiatry at Yale University School of Medicine and director of the Yale Child Study Center, recruited James P. Comer to head the initiative that would become SDP.

Around this time, Albert Solnit, Joseph Goldstein, and Anna Freud brought their unique backgrounds to the task of developing an approach of how to apply the best interests of the child standard to modern society, particularly in child custody cases and child placement decisions. In 1973, Goldstein, Freud, and Solnit published *Beyond the Best Interests of the Child*. In 1979, they published *Before the Best Interests of the Child*. Goldstein was then Sterling Professor of Law at the Yale University Law School and Yale Child Study Center. Freud was then director of the Hampstead Child-Therapy Clinic and a frequent visiting lecturer at the Yale Law School and the Yale University School of Medicine.

In law, a judge uses the best-interests standard when two parents contest their child's custody or when a foster or government agency attempts to remove a child from a family. To make a decision in the best interests of the child is to apply a legal standard that has its origins in the English court system. In the United States, Judge Benjamin Cardozo affirmed the best-interests standard in *Finlay v. Finlay*, a 1925 custody case. In custody cases, Cardozo noted, the judge should consider "what is best for the interests of the child"—and not whether father or mother "has a cause of action against the other" (*Finlay*, 240 N.Y. at 433, 148 N.E. at 626).

In *Before the Best Interests of the Child*, Goldstein, Freud, and Solnit examine when and why children's relationships to their parents become a matter of state concern. "The court is obligated by statute . . . to make the child's interests paramount—to favor the child," they wrote (p. 123). To "pour content into the best interests standard," they state that placement decisions (1) should safeguard the child's need for continuity of relationships; (2) should reflect the child's, not the adult's, sense of time; and (3) "must take into account the law's incapacity to supervise interpersonal relationships and the limits of the knowledge to make long-range predictions" (p. 6).

This content is consistent with SDP's insistence on relationships and applying knowledge of child and youth development to education. In SDP school communities, the teams use the best-interests standard when making decisions for whole schools of children. The recognition that there are limits to the knowledge of how to make accurate long-range predictions has been translated into SDP's insistence on a data-driven process of educational change. Every decision must be monitored and modified, if need be.

WHAT IS ACTUALLY INVOLVED IN MAKING A DECISION IN THE BEST INTERESTS OF CHILDREN?

In SDP school communities, decisions are made by the three teams that are the hallmark of the Comer Process: the School Planning and Management Team (SPMT), the Parent Team (PT), and the Student and Staff Support Team (SSST). The collaborative process is essential in order not to paralyze the principal, who is the legal representative of the school.

Decisions are made when change is being considered. At those times, certain notions, attitudes, and skills are also needed. It is worth listing these things because if any of them is lacking, the likely outcome will not be a decision; it will be a default. To make a decision that leads to well-managed change, people must

Be able to recognize that there should be alternatives to the current situation. If people do not have the ability to look at their situation from the outside, they will not even notice that the current situation needs to be changed. Looking in from the outside is one of the most important skills taught by SDP facilitators.

Be able to recognize that there can be alternatives to the current situation. If people have no hope, they will not even notice that the current situation can be changed.

Accept that it is possible for them to develop such alternatives. If people are not encouraged—either by their own past successes or by supportive mentors— they are not likely to apply themselves to changing.

Have the skills to conceive of and develop the details of the alternatives. If people do not know how to brainstorm and investigate without bitter argument, and if they don't know how to organize the thoughts they come up with, they will not be able to develop a coherent plan for change.

Be willing to choose between the alternatives they have developed. If people are fearful of any institutional or personal consequences of making a decision, they will not decide; they will postpone.

Know of at least one process for making such a choice. If people have alternatives but no choice process, they will become overwhelmed and avoid choosing among potential decisions.

Have the skills to use that choice process. If people are unskilled at using the choice process, the problems they encounter will either derail the process or result in such a chilling effect that future decisions will be postponed until there is a crisis that cannot be ignored.

Whether the decisions are being made by a formerly abusive parent collaborating with an SSST that is teaching her how to nurture her child, or are being made by an SPMT that is formulating a Comprehensive School Plan, all these pieces of the process are essential. (The additional notions, attitudes, and skills necessary to turn any decision into appropriate, well-monitored action are discussed in detail in each chapter of this field guide.)

DOES SERVING THE BEST INTERESTS OF CHILDREN NECESSARILY MEAN *NOT* SERVING THE INTERESTS OF ADULTS?

In many instances, adults' agendas are in direct opposition to what will promote children's healthy growth, development, and learning. In these instances, serving the children does, indeed, mean *not* serving the adults. It is not okay for a principal to hide in his or her office, for teachers to ignore abusive language or substandard practices that they observe in a colleague's classroom, for bullying to be permitted in the lunchroom or on the school yard or in a classroom because no one seems to notice it, for a family in the school to go hungry or homeless. The actions taken in the best interests of the children in these cases may even cause a staff member or administrator to be fired or cause a parent to lose custody of a child.

In most instances, however, adults' agendas are not truly in direct opposition to what will promote children's healthy growth, development, and learning, despite behavior that may range from being unhelpful to being obstructionist. In those instances, it is important to discover what positive intentions underlie (sometimes unconsciously) the negative behavior (Bateson, 1972/2000; Dilts, 1999; O'Connor & Seymour, 1990). The most efficient way to get people to change their behavior and cooperate is to make it clear that by meeting the children's needs they will satisfy their own most important needs, as well.

REFERENCES

Bateson, G. (1972/2000). *Steps to an ecology of mind.* Chicago: University of Chicago Press.

Dilts, R. (1999). *Sleight of mouth: The magic of conversational belief change.* Capitola, CA: Meta Publications.

Goldstein, J., Freud, A., & Solnit, A. J. (1973). *Beyond the best interests of the child.* New York: Free Press.

Goldstein, J., Freud, A., & Solnit, A. J. (1979). *Before the best interests of the child.* New York: Free Press.

O'Connor, J., & Seymour, J. (1990). *Introducing NLP: Neurolinguistic programming: Psychological skills for understanding and influencing people.* London/San Francisco: Thorsons/HarperCollins.

6

Designing the Comprehensive School Plan

Valerie Maholmes

The central task of the School Planning and Management Team (SPMT) is creating, supporting, and reassessing the Comprehensive School Plan (CSP). The CSP addresses every aspect of school life, and in clear, well-organized steps, this chapter addresses every aspect of designing the CSP. A case study and training activities are included as models, along with a comprehensive checklist to assure that all tasks are accomplished.

This chapter describes how to develop a Comprehensive School Plan (CSP). It also helps School Planning and Management Team (SPMT) members understand their role in creating and updating the CSP, and it discusses how to begin applying the six developmental pathways to the CSP process.

OVERVIEW OF THE THREE OPERATIONS

The SPMT designs and implements the CSP, periodically assesses how well the goals in the plan are being met, modifies the plan accordingly, and ensures that the appropriate staff development activities are aligned with the goals in the plan.

Designing the Comprehensive School Plan

The CSP is central to a school's improvement process because it sets the direction and focus for the school. Its position on the "schoolhouse" graphic of the Comer Process illustrates how central it is in helping the school community to achieve its desired outcomes (see Figure 2.2 in Chapter 2). The CSP involves more than charting progress in discrete areas of academic achievement. It promotes a thorough examination of the school as a whole. Focusing on curriculum, instruction and assessment, on academic and psychosocial goals, and on public relations and communications strategies, the CSP enables the school to target with greater accuracy the factors that underlie school performance and achievement. Thus, through establishing and updating the CSP, the school sets goals and objectives that place child development at the center of the planning process. And because these goals and objectives are supported by routinely gathered data about the whole school, they are timely, measurable, and achievable.

It is important that the CSP serve as a means for the school to communicate its priorities to the broader school community: parents, the central office, university partners, service providers, and other stakeholders. Since the SPMT completes the plan using the collaborative decision-making process, the content reflects the values of the school community as well as academic theories and assumptions about school change. Stakeholders and well-wishers need to be aware of the direction the school is taking so that they can provide necessary resources as well as cooperation and encouragement. It is very important for the members of the SPMT to distribute the CSP to their constituent groups to ensure that everyone knows and supports the focus, direction, and actions the school is taking.

Periodic Assessment and Modification

Periodic assessment and modification of the plan allows the SPMT to systematically answer the questions: "What are we doing?" "Why are we doing it?" "Which processes and strategies are working well?" "Which are not?" "What needs to be changed?" Assessing the plan involves taking an extensive look at student data on such issues as achievement, attendance, behavior, and socio-economic background.

The SPMT must also systematically collect and examine data on how the curriculum is being implemented, as well as data on how the SDP process is functioning and the impact it is having on the school. These data include perceptions of (1) school climate and academic focus, (2) implementation of the aligned and balanced curriculum, and (3) how well the nine elements of the Comer Process are being implemented. The SPMT should conduct a monthly "process check" to ensure that the activities are being carried out according to the specifications in the plan. This allows the team to keep on track and to prevent important activities from falling through the cracks. The process check also enables the team to observe and monitor targeted initiatives and activities to help determine whether they will result in the desired outcomes. Every three months, the SPMT should determine whether to continue with certain initiatives or activities, make changes, or discontinue them altogether. Of course, this assessment should be based on data. This process can begin at the subcommittee level and then be brought to the SPMT for review.

Staff Development

To provide the skills and knowledge needed to carry out the activities in the plan, staff development must be linked to the specific action steps to ensure that all parties involved have the skills and knowledge they need. The various staff development activities should involve every staff member in the school. These activities can range from sessions that teach educators how to help parents learn to support reading initiatives at home, to sessions for cafeteria staff on the connection between nutrition and learning, to specific training in teaching a particular content area. By doing this, schools create a culture of ongoing reflection and renewal. Also, schools build capacity to sustain the practices that support student learning and development.

GETTING STARTED: PREPARING TO PLAN

In getting started, the first steps are to (1) assemble the team, (2) formally schedule time in the school calendar, and (3) compile and prepare the data for review. These preparatory activities help to get the CSP process off to a positive start. By taking care to do advance planning and preparation, the SPMT can lead the school in a fruitful and productive planning process.

Assemble the Team

The most important first step in preparing for the planning process is to ensure that the SPMT has been established and that there is adequate representation from all the constituencies in the school. This is important because the goals, objectives, and strategies of the plan should reflect the collective input and wisdom of the entire school community. This is sometimes a challenge—particularly if in the past the plan was completed by the principal or by a small committee. To overcome this challenge, the SPMT chair may want to outline the tasks of the planning process and then poll the members of the team to determine their interests, skills, and the time they have available to take on these tasks. For example, there is always someone on the team who has a penchant for details and who enjoys managing the finer points of pulling the plan together. There is usually a person who enjoys working with data and who will be willing to lead the process of preparing the elements of data that will be discussed during the planning period. Of critical importance is the person who can be relied upon to complete the clerical tasks of the process and who may be willing to manage the final production of the plan itself.

In addition to these roles and responsibilities, all team members should be prepared to discuss the priorities, concerns, and suggestions raised by the group they represent and to keep their group informed of decisions and progress made.

To make sure that the process covers all these bases, use Figure 6.1, Comprehensive School Plan checklist.

Schedule Time in the School Calendar

From the outset, it is critically important that time be scheduled for the planning process. An SPMT usually meets before or after school for its regularly scheduled

Figure 6.1 Comprehensive School Plan checklist

Item	Comment
1. <u>Representation</u>: Does the plan reflect the collective input of all stakeholders?	
Teachers by grade level/specialization	☐
Administration	☐
Student and Staff Support Team (SSST) members	☐
Parent Team (PT) members	☐
Other school-based support staff	☐
Community representative(s)	☐
Before-school program staff	☐
After-school program staff	☐
Relevant other(s)	☐
2. <u>Focus (content)</u>: Does the plan put forth priorities that lead to positive student achievement and development outcomes?	
State-mandated priorities	☐
School-based priorities	☐
Classroom-based priorities	☐
3a. <u>Data sources, Part I</u>: Is the plan informed by multiple sources of data?	
Student achievement and performance	☐
SSST global patterns and trends	☐
Parent observations	☐
Community observations	☐
Student and staff perceptions	☐
Student and staff attendance	☐
School readiness including health and nutrition	☐
Family needs assessment	☐
Community needs assessment	☐
Program evaluation	☐
3b. <u>Data sources, Part II</u>: Are these data used to pinpoint priorities and desired outcomes?	
Student achievement and performance	☐
SSST global patterns and trends	☐
Parent observations	☐

Community observations	☐
Student and staff perceptions	☐
Student and staff attendance	☐
School readiness including health and nutrition	☐
Family needs assessment	☐
Community needs assessment	☐
Program evaluation	☐

4. **Format: Is the plan user friendly, an effective communications tool, and action oriented?**

Has glossary of terms	☐
Explains data sources	☐
Lists specific action steps and persons responsible for them	☐
Is easily understood by partners and lay persons	☐

5a. **Alignment, Part I: Is each objective relevantly linked to the goal(s)?**

Objective 1:	☐
Objective 2:	☐
Objective 3:	☐

5b. **Alignment, Part II: Is each action step linked to the relevant objective(s)?**

Action Step 1:	☐
Action Step 2:	☐
Action Step 3:	☐

meetings. However, during the planning period, much more time will be needed than is usually allocated for meetings. If the plan has been assessed and modified during the course of the year, then time needs to be dedicated to reviewing the outcomes of the modifications and determining which direction to take for the next academic year. On the average, most schools schedule three SPMT meetings to

- set the tone and agenda and assign roles and tasks for the planning process
- review the data and hear subcommittee, grade level, and community reports
- reach final consensus on the desired goals, objectives, and strategies

Since most of the work of achieving initial consensus and identifying priorities is done at the committee level, time also needs to be set aside to ensure that these meetings take place and that staff members have sufficient time to work through the issues.

Compile and Prepare the Data for Review

The CSP process is cyclical in nature in that it begins and ends with a thorough analysis of the data. To get started, the SPMT needs to compile all the data that will inform the decision-making process. This includes data on achievement, attendance, suspensions, mobility, referrals and social service, school climate, and anything else that is relevant. Since data often are not available to the school in the most useful form, before discussions commence the SPMT needs to take time to sort out the most important data and to prepare it so that it can facilitate discussions. If too much information is provided at once, team members may become overwhelmed rather than informed by the data.

To assist in the data collection process, use Figure 6.2, data collection and management grid.

Figure 6.2 Data collection and management grid (sample worksheet)

Discuss the current status of your school: *(A) What issues and concerns are **most important** to address? (B) What data do you have to substantiate and challenge your concerns? (C) What additional data do you need? (D) From what source can you obtain the data?*

	Issues and Concerns	Data We Have	Data We Need	Data Source
Academic				
Behavioral				
Child Development				
School or Classroom Climate				
Other				

INITIATING THE PLANNING PROCESS: SIX ESSENTIAL STEPS

The six essential steps in the CSP process are (1) establish or revisit the vision, (2) introduce child development into the planning process, (3) identify goals and priorities, (4) establish an action plan, (5) review and finalize the plan with the team, and (6) distribute the plan to all stakeholders. Then it is time to celebrate the work that was accomplished and honor the journey ahead.

Establish or Revisit the Vision

An essential step in initiating the planning process is either establishing or revisiting the school's vision. Remember that the CSP communicates what you value as a school community—it reflects the philosophy that guides your approach to school improvement. The plan is not only a document that lists a series of goals and activities, but in many ways it is a narrative describing the school's evolution—where you've been and where you see yourselves heading. Thus the vision statement should reflect the essence and intent of the planned experiences and how these experiences will promote students' learning and development. Revisiting the vision statement helps bring the school together around the important ideals and principles of the broader school community. This is important, particularly if there have been major staff or administrative changes or if the demographics of the population typically served by the school have changed in any significant way. Finally, the process of visioning helps the staff, parents, students, and community achieve consensus on new directions and helps define the scope of change they wish to take on. The following examples of vision statements reflect these ideas:

> We will work as a team in a trusting environment where every student will be treated with dignity, experience success, and have access to caring and supportive adults.

> The faculty and staff at Emma Francis Grayson Merritt Elementary Extended School are committed to individual and collective responsibility for lifelong learning and see children as critical to the community and the city's success. All our daily interactions are influenced by the belief that equitable opportunities should exist for all.

> The community of Emma E. Booker Elementary School recognizes that students enter school with different backgrounds and experiences. It is our belief that all children can be successful when accepted at their level of development. By holding high expectations for parents, students, teachers, and administrators and by using a no-fault approach, we believe we can lead every child toward becoming a productive and successful member of society.

In the space provided below, write your school's current vision statement.

Our School's Vision

_____

_____

_____

_____

What does the statement say about your school in terms of its basic ideals and the philosophy that guides the work of the school? In what ways can you broaden the scope of the vision? What are the implications for your school plan? Will the goals in your plan help your school move toward its vision? How will you communicate this vision to the broader school community?

Introduce Child Development Into the Planning Process

Once the school has achieved consensus on its vision, it is important to examine the extent to which the activities and programs address the six developmental pathways in a balanced way. School plans typically focus on the school's instructional goals, and consequently the balance of programs is often tipped toward the cognitive pathway. A purpose of the Comer Process CSP is to ensure that there is adequate programming to address students' needs along each of the pathways. By doing so, the school creates a child development–centered educational agenda so that students have the best possible chance of being successful.

To get started with this phase of the planning process, the SPMT subcommittees take an inventory of the school's current programs and activities and examine whether the offerings are developmentally balanced and serve the needs of all the students. Before any goals, objectives, or new programs are established, the SPMT conducts this analysis using the format shown in Figure 6.3.

First list all the programs that support the curriculum. These include programs and activities that are offered before, during, and after school such as supplemental curriculum initiatives, after-school tutorial programs, behavioral intervention programs, and the like. Next, determine which students are being served by the programs and any special characteristics the programs are designed to address (e.g., low math achievement, self-esteem for girls). Finally, indicate which pathways are being addressed. The pathways are interactive—not discrete—so you may find that a particular program or activity addresses more than one pathway. However, be careful to check no more than two primary pathways targeted by the activity. In doing this analysis be sure to focus on the primary aims of the program.

Once the inventory for introducing child development is complete, the subcommittees should bring their work back to the SPMT and prepare the data for analysis, using the following questions as a guide:

Figure 6.3   Inventory for introducing child development (sample worksheet)

Programs	Grade	Gender (M/F)	Target Population	Physical	Cognitive	Psychological	Language	Social	Ethical
	Students Served			**Developmental Pathways**					
Mastery test preparation	7th	Males	Students who fall below basic achievement levels in math and science	✓	✓		✓		
Read Alouds	7th and 8th	Males/ females	Students reading below grade level		✓		✓		
Raisin'-up Club	7th	Males/ females	All students			✓		✓	✓

- To what extent are our programs balanced developmentally?
- On which pathways do we focus most?
- On which pathways do we focus least?
- Which students are being served by our programs and activities?
- Are there programs for high-achieving as well as low-achieving students?
- Do the programs primarily target boys or girls?
- Are any of the programs and activities redundant?

Answers to these questions should help the SPMT identify developmental and programmatic priorities and get a clearer picture of goals and objectives that need to be established.

Identify Goals and Priorities

Once all the analyses have been completed and data collected and prioritized, the SPMT can begin formulating the goals for the CSP. Most often the district sets targeted goal areas, but the schools can establish subordinate goals that reflect the needs of the specific building. For example, if the district goal is to improve mathematics achievement, then the SPMT should review the mathematics data at their school and identify specific skill and content areas that need to be addressed. Based on findings from the inventory and other data sources, the SPMT may also choose to craft goals that target a specific group of students (e.g., third-grade boys). Each goal should reflect a broad statement of intent that relates to a particular area of need and articulates the desired trend or outcome.

CSPs should also look beyond the specially targeted problem areas to include other goals, so that both ongoing programs and innovative ideas that the school may want to pilot are managed by the SPMT. Use the questions below as a guide to formulate problem solving, maintenance, or innovative goals.

1. Problem solving:
   In which area(s) is performance not up to standard?
   How much measurable improvement is realistic at this time?

2. Maintenance:
   What have been the benefits of our current approach?
   What will it take in terms of time and resources to continue these efforts?
   How will we monitor our activities?

3. Innovative:
   What new ideas do we want to implement?
   What will be the measurable, added benefits?
   What will it cost to generate these benefits?

Establish an Action Plan

The action plan helps keep the CSP a living document. So, in addition to the goals, objectives, and activities, the SPMT must also specify how the activities will be accomplished, who will be responsible, and how the activities will be funded, publicized, and evaluated. To organize this information, use Figure 6.4, the comprehensive school plan matrix.

Review and Finalize the Plan With the Team

Before the SPMT gives the CSP its seal of approval, an important step in the planning process is to give the plan a final review to ensure that there is consensus on its direction and focus. This review should be done by the entire SPMT so that parents, teachers, administrators, staff, and students have the opportunity to make adjustments, clarify roles and responsibilities, or express final concerns. The CSP checklist (Figure 6.1) can be used as a guide to facilitate this review.

Distribute the Plan to All Stakeholders and Celebrate the Journey

After the plan has been completed and the SPMT has achieved consensus on its direction and focus, the final document should be distributed to the broader school community so that everyone can have the opportunity to see the outcome of their work. Remember: The CSP represents the collective values, hopes, and dreams of the school community, so it's really important to find an opportunity to celebrate the journey! Think of creative ways to acknowledge the work of the members of the team who have shared their time and talent to design the plan. Most important, celebrate the students as they accomplish significant developmental milestones and make significant academic strides. Success breeds success—every movement toward the goal, no matter how small, is worthy of celebration!

Figure 6.4 Comprehensive school plan matrix (sample worksheet)

Goal:

Objective:

Developmental Pathways Addressed:

Action Step	Budget Funding Source	Person or Team Responsible	Timeline		Staff and Adult Development Needed	Resources Needed	Indicators and Benchmarks	Communications and Public Relations Strategy
			Start	Finish				

STARTING THE ASSESSMENT AND MODIFICATION PROCESS

The comprehensive school planning process requires a lot of time and attention to detail, which can be overwhelming if the planning and preparation steps listed in this chapter haven't been taken into account. Because this is a time-intensive process, it is also important to break the activities down into doable steps that can be carried out during the school year. Figure 6.5, the comprehensive school plan implementation timeline, is a guide to help SPMTs focus their efforts to get the most out of their time together. Also included in the timeline are critical questions that need to be addressed every three months as part of the CSP assessment and modification process.

PLANNING PRACTICE USING THE FISK MIDDLE SCHOOL CASE STUDY

The ideas presented in this chapter will help your SPMT design a CSP that will enable the school to accomplish its goals and achieve desired outcomes. To get

Figure 6.5 Comprehensive school plan implementation timeline

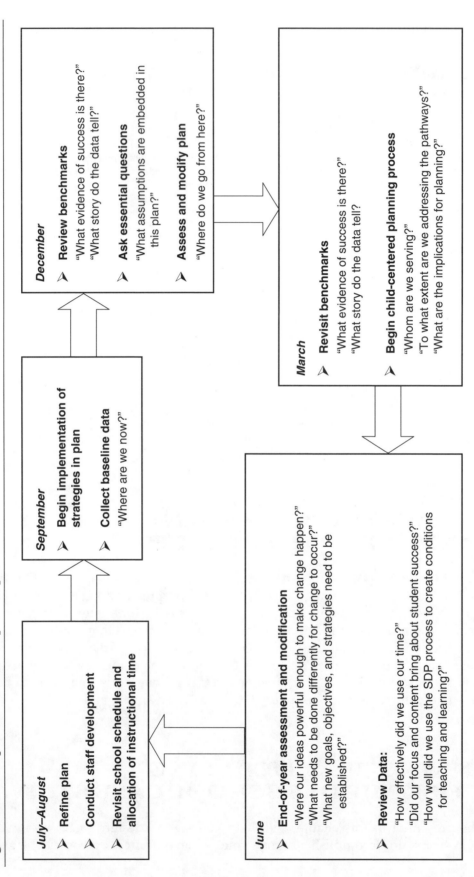

July–August
> Refine plan
> Conduct staff development
> Revisit school schedule and allocation of instructional time

September
> **Begin implementation of strategies in plan**
> **Collect baseline data**
  "Where are we now?"

December
> **Review benchmarks**
  "What evidence of success is there?"
  "What story do the data tell?"
> **Ask essential questions**
  "What assumptions are embedded in this plan?"
> **Assess and modify plan**
  "Where do we go from here?"

March
> **Revisit benchmarks**
  "What evidence of success is there?"
  "What story do the data tell?
> **Begin child-centered planning process**
  "Whom are we serving?"
  "To what extent are we addressing the pathways?"
  "What are the implications for planning?"

June
> **End-of-year assessment and modification**
  "Were our ideas powerful enough to make change happen?"
  "What needs to be done differently for change to occur?"
  "What new goals, objectives, and strategies need to be established?"
> **Review Data:**
  "How effectively did we use our time?"
  "Did our focus and content bring about student success?"
  "How well did we use the SDP process to create conditions for teaching and learning?"

68

your SPMT on the right track in this process, use the Fisk Middle School case study (pseudonymous composite) presented below as part of staff development activities. This will give the team the opportunity to practice some of the planning activities before they undertake the actual planning process. Good luck!

The Case Study

Background

Fisk Middle School is a Grade 5–Grade 8 school located in Fisk Community, an inner city in the Midwest. The school's student body is comprised of African Americans (30 percent), Latinos (35 percent), Native Americans (15 percent), European Americans (15 percent), and Asian Americans (5 percent). Most of the students live in the community; however, a small percentage (20 percent) are children of industrial workers who commute from the outskirts of town.

The faculty and staff are predominantly European American (55 percent) and African American (30 percent); Latinos and Native Americans account for 10 percent and 5 percent, respectively.

Until recently, Fisk Community was a thriving industrial center that employed residents of ethnically diverse communities from within a 25-mile radius. Many of the industry's employees are speakers of other languages and rarely find it necessary to socialize with fellow employees from different ethnic backgrounds. Fisk Community is a working-class city with residents sometimes having two jobs; the commuters work long hours, making it difficult for them to attend functions at their children's school. Only a small percentage of the Fisk Community residents are upper middle class. Their children usually attend private schools.

Due to a downward trend in the economy, cutbacks in working hours and benefits were made at the industrial center seven years ago. Many of the jobs were "upgraded" and moved to suburban communities. Some employees, especially the commuters, had to find other ways to supplement their income. Others enrolled in job training programs in the hope that they would be considered for a job upgrade. Those whose proficiency in English was limited found it necessary to work at becoming proficient in English.

The Problem

Over the past three decades, the mission of Fisk Middle School has been to prepare students to be contributing members of Fisk Community. Basic skills in all subjects were taught, as well as foreign languages, home economics, and vocational technical studies. It was generally expected that most students, after graduation from high school, would work in one of the industrial shops. The school began implementing SDP a year prior to the economic downshift. As a result of SDP implementation, most faculty and staff felt that there was a relatively good climate in the school. Commuting students were bused in at 7:35 a.m. and bused out at 3:45 p.m.; students tended to socialize at recess with other students from their own ethnic group. Only a few classrooms initiated activities that would require students to interact with students from other groups. For the most part, students seemed to be well-behaved, no racial problems were evident, and everyone seemed to get along well with each other.

With the economic downshift, the administration began to observe changes in the overall climate at Fisk Middle School. The SPMT asked the Assessment and Modification Subcommittee to use action research strategies to clarify the situation. They decided to administer SDP's school climate surveys, observe classrooms, and collect student data. Upon completion of the investigation, the subcommittee submitted a report to the SPMT. About one month later, the SPMT called an emergency meeting to review the data and address the issues at hand. What follows is the executive summary of the subcommittee's report.

Executive Summary: Submitted by the Fisk Middle School Assessment and Modification Subcommittee

Child Development Findings for the Month of April

The monthly statistics for this school year show that student enrollment and attendance and participation declined. There seems to be a higher incidence of dropouts, particularly males, at Grade 8. Students who commuted to the school appeared to be absent and tardy more frequently than other students were. At the lower grade levels, there also appeared to be increasingly more competition among students for teachers' attention and less cooperative classroom behavior. In class, students tended to tease and make jokes about students from other ethnic groups because of their speech patterns or appearance. During focus group interviews, teachers complained of having difficulty affirming and addressing the needs of such a diverse student population. It was also noted that teachers were having to make more referrals than usual to the Student and Staff Support Team (SSST) for inappropriate behavior. For example, some of the teachers reported that students, especially the commuters, began eating their lunches during class time and that some students were falling asleep in class, while others seemed distracted, especially toward the end of the school day. (Some data that support these findings appear in Table 6.1.)

Adult and Student Relationship Findings

During focus group interviews with randomly selected students from each grade level, it was noted that students reported difficulties their families were facing at work and at home. The commuting students felt that neither their teachers nor their parents understood what they were going through and as a result found it difficult to concentrate on their studies. Some teachers indicated that they have attempted to involve parents, but to no avail (see Table 6.2). As a result, there seemed to be low morale among the teaching staff and a diminished sense of job satisfaction.

Table 6.1   Fisk Middle School performance data

Total number of school days: 180   **Total number of students:** 245

Grade Level	Number of Days Absent		Number of Times Tardy		Number of Special Education Referrals		Number of Behavioral Referrals	
	Male	Female	Male	Female	Male	Female	Male	Female
Fifth Grade	20	6	39	20	15	5	27	12
Sixth Grade	36	17	45	15	11	7	35	8
Seventh Grade	30	15	40	19	9	5	48	9
Eighth Grade	51	27	49	33	00	2	35	15

Grade Level	Total Number of Retentions		Total Number of Dropouts	
	Male	Female	Male	Female
Fifth Grade	0	0	0	0
Sixth Grade	1	0	0	0
Seventh Grade	3	1	2	0
Eight Grade	0	1	17	5

Table 6.2   Fisk Middle School parent involvement data

Grade Level	Number of PTO/PTA Members		Number of Parent Volunteers in School	
	Male	*Female*	*Male*	*Female*
Fifth Grade	2	10	5	12
Sixth Grade	0	16	3	7
Seventh Grade	0	7	0	3
Eighth Grade	3	6	0	0

The students also reported that teachers were asking them to learn things in school that didn't seem to be relevant to what they would need once they left school. Finally, all the students agreed that they would like to know more about students from other backgrounds, especially since their parents were being exposed to other cultures through their interactions at work. However, teachers complained about having to integrate multicultural activities into their lessons, indicating that "the students have always gotten along well with each other; these problems will pass when the economy gets better."

Curriculum and Instruction Findings

With regard to the curriculum, more students were enrolled in the vocational technical programs than in the academic programs. Standardized tests revealed that the female fifth-grade students were at or above grade level for language arts, math, and reading. However, the male students were only at grade level for language arts. Eighth-grade students were above grade level in language arts but below grade level in reading. In terms of math achievement, the male students were at grade level but the female students were slightly below. (The data that support these findings appear in Table 6.3.)

Faithful Replication Issues

The SDP Process Documentation Inventory (PDI) was completed by constituent groups at the school. Findings showed that most of the groups strongly disagreed that "the SSST develops preventive strategies that create optimum conditions for teaching and learning." Groups also disagreed with the statement that parents were viewed as partners in developing programs and interventions for students. In addition, the findings revealed that the SPMT does not monitor the Comprehensive School Plan, nor does the group send home a copy of the plan to parents. Most constituent groups also felt that people were not taking risks because of the concern that they would be blamed if something went wrong.

Table 6.3   Fisk Middle School achievement outcomes

| | Grade Equivalent Scores | | | | | |
| | Language | | Math | | Reading | |
Grade Level	Male	Female	Male	Female	Male	Female
Fifth Grade	5.5	6.0	4.7	5.0	4.3	5.1
Sixth Grade	6.3	6.7	5.8	5.5	5.0	4.7
Seventh Grade	7.0	7.5	6.7	7.1	6.8	7.0
Eighth Grade	8.5	8.5	8.0	7.5	7.0	7.5

Staff Development Activity 6.1: Analyzing the Data Collection Process

The Fisk SPMT called an emergency meeting to review the Assessment and Modification Subcommittee's report, but they had difficulty making sense of all the data and initiating the planning process. The role of the SPMT in the planning process is to bring members of the team to consensus on the issues of data gathering. The kinds of data the school collects, the sources from which data are obtained, and the methods used to collect the data should support the question or problem the school wishes to address.

Take a few minutes to familiarize yourselves with the data in Tables 6.1, 6.2, and 6.3. Review the Fisk Middle School case again and answer the following questions:

1. What kinds of data were collected?

_____

_____

_____

2. What counted as data? What were the data sources?

_____

_____

_____

3. What methods were used to collect the data?

_____

_____

_____

4. Which developmental pathway(s) did the data address?

_____

_____

_____

Staff Development Activity 6.2:
Defining the Issues and Making Meaning

Let's see if we can make meaning out of the Fisk Middle School data. Making meaning out of data is a challenging yet critical aspect of the planning process. Disaggregating (breaking down) the data to highlight specific group characteristics allows you to clearly define the pertinent issues and pinpoint the groups with whom interventions need to be made. Select a data table and answer the following questions:

1. What questions come to mind as you review the table?

    _____

    _____

    _____

    _____

2. What issues or concerns does the data table raise?

    _____

    _____

    _____

    _____

3. What additional information is needed?

    _____

    _____

    _____

    _____

Reflect:

- What are the advantages and disadvantages of breaking down or disaggregating the data?
- On what other group characteristics could you disaggregate these data?
- Do the observations and interviews support the numerical data?

    _____

    _____

    _____

    _____

Staff Development Activity 6.3:
Choosing the Essential Questions for
Designing the Comprehensive School Plan

For this staff development activity, act as if you were the Fisk SPMT. Review the data and answer the following questions:

1. Clarify process and outcomes.
   What did the staff, students, and parents at Fisk do? (process)
   What seemed to happen as a result? (outcomes)

2. Define the critical issues revealed in the data.
   What is the big picture?
   What story do the data tell?

3. Determine priorities.
   What issues seem to require immediate attention?
   What issues seem to require additional planning, clarification, etc.?

Now that you have reviewed the Fisk Middle School data, brainstorm possible goals the Fisk SPMT should consider putting in its comprehensive plan for problem solving, maintenance, and innovation.

4. List suggestions for problem-solving goals.

   _____

   _____

   _____

5. List suggestions for maintenance goals.

   _____

   _____

   _____

6. List suggestions for innovative goals.

   _____

   _____

   _____

READ MORE ABOUT . . .

To read more about SDP's approach to assessment, see "Assessing Systemic Reform," Chapter 17 in *Dynamic Instructional Leadership to Support Student Learning and Development: The Field Guide to Comer Schools in Action* in this series.

School Planning and Management Team (SPMT) Subcommittees

Where the Work of the Comprehensive School Plan Gets Done

**Malcolm N. Adler and Jan Stocklinski
with contributions by J. Patrick Howley,
Sherrie Berrien Joseph, and the Comer Staff
of Prince George's County Public Schools, Maryland**

Decades of experience have produced a deep and broad knowledge base that is distilled here in the form of discussions, guidelines, strategies, and checklists. This detailed and comprehensive treatment will support both new and experienced School Planning and Management Teams (SPMTs) as they create or refine their subcommittee structure and will support the subcommittees as they carry out the Comprehensive School Plan.

SUBCOMMITTEE BASICS

Each school needs to create subcommittees to carry out the work of the Comprehensive School Plan. We recommend that each School Planning and Management Team (SPMT) have a subcommittee for each of the following areas:

- curriculum, instruction, and assessment
- climate
- adult development and training (for staff and parents)
- public relations
- grade-level teams
- student government

Schools may have more subcommittees, but they should be mindful of keeping them to a manageable number.

Staff members and family members are strongly encouraged to serve on at least one subcommittee. This increases the likelihood that each subcommittee will represent as many different school stakeholders as possible. For example, we recommend the following people serve on the Curriculum, Instruction, and Assessment (CIA) Subcommittee: teachers and instructional assistants at different grade levels, parents, and appropriate specialists based in a school. Too often, we have seen schools in which there are 20 people on the Climate Subcommittee and only five people on the CIA Subcommittee. Subcommittees need to have a cross-section of members representing the whole school community. Subcommittee size will vary depending on the size of the school. The larger the subcommittee, the greater the need for operating with cooperative learning strategies. See Figure 7.1 for other practical strategies for guiding the work of the subcommittees.

Subcommittees need to meet at the beginning of the school year—or even before school begins—to decide how they will operate for the year (e.g., roles and ground rules, times and dates of meetings) and when they will review the Comprehensive School Plan. In this way, they will be clear regarding their responsibilities.

It is critical that a representative from each subcommittee participate actively on the SPMT to ensure healthy communication between the SPMT and the subcommittees. Concise reports of the subcommittees should be shared at SPMT meetings (and in the publicly posted minutes of those meetings). Some schools place a notebook with all meeting agendas and notes in the front office. This is highly recommended. All teams and subcommittees in the school should be trained in using a "positive problem-solving strategy" when faced with challenging issues (see Figure 7.2).

> Subcommittees should have some members who are not serving on the SPMT.
>
> Subcommittee chairs should be SPMT members.

Each SPMT subcommittee works to carry out specific goals and objectives identified in the Comprehensive School Plan. The following description of subcommittee responsibilities is a compilation of materials developed by the Yale School Development Program, and by Washington School in Camden, New Jersey.

Figure 7.1 Strategies for guiding the work of subcommittees, constituency groups, and teams: A decision-making process

1. Identify the issue(s) to be addressed: What is the central or core issue? Define or redefine the core issue by looking at it from various perspectives. For example, how might other groups perceive this issue?

2. Develop a proposed program and strategies. Brainstorm all alternative strategies for addressing the core issue.

3. List questions that you have for each strategy. Do not answer them—get all the questions on the table.

4. List the advantages of each strategy.

5. List the disadvantages of each strategy.

6. List and prioritize recommendations.

7. Write your thinking process and rationale for each recommendation.

8. Get input and/or agreement on the proposed program or strategy(ies). This should include input from the administrators, staff, parents, or any person or group impacted by the proposed program or strategy(ies).

9. Bring the proposed program or strategy(ies) to the full SPMT. Add, question, decide.

10. Implement the agreed-upon program or strategy(ies).

11. Monitor and assess the implementation.

12. Make modifications as needed.

SOURCE: J. Patrick Howley and Sherrie B. Joseph.

CURRICULUM, INSTRUCTION, AND ASSESSMENT SUBCOMMITTEE

The responsibilities of the CIA Subcommittee are (1) to clarify for the entire school community the connections among curriculum, instruction, relationships, and youth development and (2) to ensure that these connections are the general focus of all work in the school. The CIA Subcommittee links the governance and management process to classroom practice by working to improve the overall academic and social functioning of the students. Although specific staff members and parents sign up for this subcommittee, the school activities, programs, and assemblies need to be planned and supported by the entire school community. All grade levels and departments need to be represented on this subcommittee.

Figure 7.2   Positive problem solving

1. Define the problem.

   The way any problem is defined sets the course for all that follows. Defining the problem is especially important because the guiding principle of no-fault can be difficult to hold onto when one is describing (and possibly reliving) problems that trigger frustration, fear, or anger.

2. Brainstorm possible solutions and promising ideas.

3. Narrow the number of possible solutions to a workable number.

4. Explore the potential positive and negative consequences of each possible solution.

5. Prioritize solutions.

6. Decide on a plan of action for your number one priority.

7. Implement the plan.

8. Evaluate the results.

   If the solution works, congratulations!
   If the solution doesn't work, go back to number 5.

Appropriate tasks for the CIA Subcommittee include the following:

- Facilitate curriculum development and the alignment of the curriculum with district and state standards.
- Examine reading, technology, and all other curricular initiatives.
- Analyze school data, test results, and grade distribution.
- Order appropriate instructional materials based on needs and data.
- Work with the Adult Development and Training Subcommittee to ensure appropriate training for staff and families in the areas of curriculum, instruction, and assessment.
- Oversee special programs that support curriculum and instruction. In particular, a task of the CIA Subcommittee is to ensure that all staff members are involved in implementation of such special programs as school assemblies, American Education Week, special month celebrations, exhibits, fairs, bees and other contests, and concerts.
- Collaborate with teachers to implement principles of youth development in the classroom.

CLIMATE SUBCOMMITTEE

The responsibilities of the Climate Subcommittee are to monitor and improve the social and emotional environment of all aspects of the school community. This environment has an impact on many aspects of students' learning and development, including self-concept, behavior, and academic achievement. School climate also impacts staff morale, feelings of empowerment, and ability to change. School climate emerges from consistent patterns in attitudes and behaviors among students, teachers, parents, administrators, and support staff. Appropriate tasks for the Climate Subcommittee include the following:

- Develop strategies to
    improve school and classroom climate,
    enhance the morale of staff, students, and parents, and
    promote students' social development.
- Oversee the administration of surveys that measure the nature and quality of school climate.
- Work with the CIA Subcommittee to interpret the data.
- Function as a social committee for staff, for example, arrange staff sympathy gifts or celebrations, organize staff social events.
- Encourage student awards and other incentives.
- When planning and organizing activities:
    reach out to all staff members and families (not just the ones on the subcommittee), and
    collaborate with staff members and families to promote their active involvement.

ADULT DEVELOPMENT AND TRAINING SUBCOMMITTEE

In some schools, this subcommittee is known as the Staff and Parent Professional Development and Training Subcommittee. This subcommittee addresses development and training for staff, parents, and families. Its responsibilities are (1) to act on the development and training implications of the goals and objectives of the Comprehensive School Plan; (2) to ensure that staff development keeps pace with district and state mandates; (3) to focus staff development on curriculum and instruction, child and adolescent development, and relationships; and (4) to increase the knowledge and skills of parents. Appropriate tasks for this subcommittee include the following:

- Analyze the development and training needs and desires of staff and parents.
- Implement the plans for training.
- Assess the value of each training event:
    Analyze evaluations to look for patterns that can guide future events.
    Analyze the impact the training had on student achievement.
    Provide feedback to the presenters.
    During the school year, suggest modifications of the staff development plan.
- Coordinate training dates on the school's master calendar.
- Maintain a staff development portfolio for the school (see Figure 7.3).
- Encourage parents to be part of the subcommittee.
- Include parents in staff professional development activities when possible or practical.

Figure 7.3 School staff development portfolio

Please note: This figure contains examples of staff development activities. This figure shows how some schools track all the training experiences in which staff members have participated over the years. They do so as a way of gaining a clear sense of identifying their current training needs.

Staff Member's Name	SDP 101 – Yale SDP	SDP 102 – Yale SDP	Literacy Training	School-based SDP Training	Inclusion Training	Specific Curriculum Training	Core Curriculum Content Standards Training	Team Training	Performance-based Assessment Training	Bilingual Education Training

- Encourage parents to present or copresent during training sessions, depending on their expertise.
- Provide opportunities for staff and parents who attend any professional development events to teach others what they have learned.
- Clarify for the school community the connections between all the staff and parent development activities and the goals identified in the Comprehensive School Plan.

PUBLIC RELATIONS SUBCOMMITTEE

The responsibilities of the Public Relations Subcommittee are (1) to coordinate the school's public relations campaign, (2) to handle requests for information on the school, (3) to provide oversight for the school newsletter, and (4) to coordinate communications with the wider community in which the school is located. Appropriate tasks for this subcommittee include the following:

- Share the school's successes with the school community and the public. This subcommittee is proactive rather than reactive in that it collaborates with the school administration to submit positive information about the school to the local press.
- Oversee the year-long school calendar. With input from the facilitator, principal, SPMT, and other subcommittees, the Public Relations Subcommittee is responsible for updating the calendar (weekly or monthly) and posting it in a prominent place in the school.
- Oversee the school newsletter. This function may vary from school to school. As a subcommittee, always keep this thought in mind: "How can students also be involved?"
- Create a one-page brochure or school profile for staff and families that includes a description of the components of the School Development Program (SDP) in the school.
- Invite politicians, central office staff, and school board members to school events (when appropriate and with approval of administration).
- Help coordinate calendar planning with feeder schools.

GRADE-LEVEL TEAMS FUNCTIONING AS SUBCOMMITTEES

Appropriate tasks for the grade-level teams include the following:

- Keep the communication flowing between members of the subcommittee and all other subcommittees.
- Work to create a curriculum that is aligned with district and state standards.
- Ensure the implementation of the newly aligned curriculum.
- Share and model best practices.
- Communicate with other grade levels on a regular basis through the SPMT.

- Plan field trips and other special events, reconciling with the master calendar.
- Share newly learned information with colleagues after attending a workshop.
- Assess and modify any grade-level curriculum programs on an ongoing basis.
- Analyze student performance on tests and disaggregate data, as appropriate (e.g., a comparison of the performance of male and female students).
- Through the SPMT, feed back what was gleaned through the assessment and modification process to other grade-level subcommittees, especially any relevant data and suggestions about their own curriculum.
- As appropriate, implement peer coaching and collaborative methods among the teachers on the grade-level team and with teachers from other grades.

STUDENT GOVERNMENT TEAM FUNCTIONING AS A SUBCOMMITTEE

Appropriate tasks for the Student Government Team include the following:

- Represent the concerns and issues of all students.
- Train students to be leaders.
- Communicate with the SPMT.
- Plan or assist in planning schoolwide student events.

ESTABLISHING AND MAINTAINING EFFECTIVE SUBCOMMITTEES

Certain aspects of subcommittee form and function are consistent, regardless of the subcommittee name. Effective subcommittees use the three guiding principles of consensus, collaboration, and no-fault to develop their organization, plan their activities, assess how well they are fulfilling their responsibilities, update their organization, and plan for the future.

Practical Tools for Establishing Effective Subcommittees

Figures 7.4 through 7.8 offer checklists and questionnaires that can help subcommittee members to establish and maintain their groups' effectiveness.

First Steps

Figure 7.4, "Questions to answer when setting up a subcommittee," supports members' progress in determining the structure of their subcommittee and the basics of communication with the school community.

Figure 7.4 Questions to answer when setting up a subcommittee

Question
1. How often will the subcommittee meet?
2. When will subcommittee meetings take place?
3. Where will subcommittee meetings take place?
4. Are these meetings scheduled on the school's master calendar?
5. Have subcommittee roles been established?
6. Is there a cochairperson to take over in case the chair is absent?
7. Have dialogue rules and meeting guidelines for the year been established?
8. How will you ensure that the three guiding principles (consensus, collaboration, and no-fault) will be practiced at each meeting?
9. Is there a meaningful agenda for each meeting?
10. Is this agenda posted __ days before each meeting in a central place for all to see?
11. How will you communicate back and forth with your constituency groups?
12. How will you communicate back and forth with the SPMT?
13. Will notes be taken of key points during these back-and-forth communications?
14. In what ways will these key points be communicated to your subcommittee?
15. As you plan events, whom will you invite?
16. Should you invite people outside of your building who support your school?
17. Are you committed to making each meeting meaningful?
18. In what specific ways will you translate this commitment into action?
19. Does everyone bring a copy of the Comprehensive School Plan with them to the meetings?

Figure 7.5   Subcommittee members' responsibilities

Responsibility
Before Each Meeting
• Reread the minutes of the previous meeting as a check of whether you have completed all assigned tasks and commitments from that meeting.
• Meet with your constituency group and have its input ready to present to the subcommittee.
• Develop agenda items in advance of the meeting.
• Bring any needed materials or data that would support agenda items.
• Plan so that you can arrive on time and stay until the end.
• If you must be absent, prepare your alternate with all needed information.
• Make arrangements to avoid being called out of the meeting by phone calls or visitors.
• Whoever is responsible: Have the room set up with tables pulled together, adequate seating, role cards, guiding principles, chart paper, and markers.
During Each Meeting
• Promote team building. Remember that each time a new person joins the team, it is a new team.
• Do a round robin: Each person on the team brings the team up to date on what has happened since the last meeting.
• Follow the ground rules that were set in the beginning of the year or the updated versions of those rules.
• Stay on the agenda and help others stay on it.
• Participate. When you have an opinion (representing your constituency group), state it honestly and clearly. Don't "sit on" feelings.
• Assume responsibility for making sure that the process of the meeting facilitates problem solving: Ask questions. Keep the group on track. Clarify members' statements. Ask for data or research.
• Summarize
• Listen attentively to others
• Use brainstorming
• Encourage everyone to speak
• Ask how this idea or strategy will make a difference for students
• Avoid communication that disrupts groups, such as sarcasm, diversions, inappropriate humor, asides, jokes, and digs.
• Think of solutions that might resolve conflicts.

• Keep notes that reflect areas of agreement.
• Keep notes that reflect who is responsible for what.
• Keep notes that reflect timelines.
• Remember that you are representing other people.
• Consider small-group discussions in order to promote a high level of active participation in the meeting by all of the members.
After Each Meeting
• Help clean up and put the room back the way you found it.
• Carry out your assignments and commitments.
• Communicate to your constituency group information that was given and decisions that were made at the meeting.
• Keep confidential anything that was said or done in the meeting—except for final decisions.
• Refrain from complaining about a decision that was agreed on at the meeting. Don't pass the buck and don't hold "parking lot" meetings.
• Refrain from out-of-meeting appeals to the leaders. Your feelings and views about the group should be expressed in the group.
• Don't appeal to the leader to reverse a decision. Bring the subject up at the next meeting.

SOURCE: This list combines the contributions of Dr. Thomas Gordon, Gordon Training International (www.thomasgordon.com), with those of the staff of the Prince George's County Comer Office and Human Relations Office. It is used here courtesy of Dr. Gordon and the Prince George's County Public Schools, Maryland. www.corwinpress.com.

Subcommittee Members' Responsibilities

Figure 7.5, "Subcommittee members' responsibilities," is a general inventory that will help members keep track of their tasks and commitments.

Planning Workshops and Trainings

Successful workshops and ongoing trainings sponsored by any subcommittee also have many aspects in common. Figure 7.6, "Questions to answer when planning workshops and trainings," is a comprehensive list that covers (1) setting the goals, objectives, and agenda; (2) attracting and communicating with participants; (3) technicalities of contracting for speakers, substitute teachers, and sites; (4) obtaining supplies; (5) arranging the training room; and (6) final details, evaluating the event, and assessing its impact.

(Text continues on page 94)

Figure 7.6 Questions to answer when planning workshops and trainings

Question
Goals, Objectives, and Agenda
• What are the goals and objectives of the workshop?
• What is the agenda?
• What are the expected outcomes?
• How will you take the developmental pathways into account?
• How will this workshop tie into the goals of your Comprehensive School Plan?
• How will this workshop tie in to your district and state goals and standards?
• Was the Staff and Parent Professional Development and Training Subcommittee involved in planning this workshop?
• Have you involved others who have attended similar training?
Attracting and Communicating With Participants
• Who is your audience?
• How many participants do you want to have?
• How much space will you need?
• Is the site climate-controlled (e.g., air-conditioned during the summer)?
• Does the announcement contain the goals, objectives, and expected outcomes of the workshop?
• Does the announcement contain pertinent information: when, how, where, cost, RSVP by when and to whom, dress, a map to the workshop site, and whether meals will be served?
• Have you developed a procedure for posting an announcement of the workshop or sending out invitations in a timely manner?
• Has the date been posted on the master calendar?
• Have copies of the announcement been sent to the appropriate school staff and central district office staff?
• Who else needs to be invited: e.g., board members, the national office of the Yale School Development Program?
• Are there other persons or offices that need to be involved in the planning or coordination?
• Are there other persons or offices that need to know that the announcement has been sent?

Question
Technicalities
• Is a contract needed? If so, who signs it and when?
• Do you need board approval and permission?
• Do you need to arrange transportation for participants?
• Do you need to arrange transportation for speakers?
• Will food be provided?
• If food will be provided, what arrangements have to be made?
• Do you need hotel arrangements?
• Who will write invitations to the speakers, and when?
• Will anything be available for sale during the workshop?
• If anything will be sold, who will handle this?
• Will you need to hire substitute teachers?
• How will substitute teachers be paid?
• How will this information about substitute teachers be communicated to the schools?
• At what time can you get to the site?
• Have you spoken with the custodial staff if they are needed?
Supplies
• What handouts will you need?
• Do handouts need to be printed or copied?
• Will you need folders or notebooks?
• Will you be providing special bags?
• Will you be providing name tags?
• Will you be making sign-in sheets?

(Continued)

Figure 7.6 (Continued)

Question
Supplies (Continued)
• Are directional signs needed in halls, at front doors, and in the parking lot?
• Have you prepared a master list of names, addresses, and phone numbers?
• Have you prepared evaluation forms or an assessment instrument?
• Have you prepared certificates for participants?
• Have you arranged for audiovisual equipment, e.g., TV and VCR and/or an overhead or computer projector for a PowerPoint presentation?
• Will you need a tape recorder and tapes and/or a CD player and CDs?
• Will you need extra bulbs and batteries for equipment?
• Will you need blank transparencies?
• Will you need chart paper and stands?
• Will you need a timer, masking tape, scissors, a stapler, or thumb tacks?
• Do you have guiding principles cards for each table as well as role cards? (See the resource section at the end of this book.)
• Will you need supplies on each table (e.g., Post-It Notes, pencils, markers)?
• Will you be providing paper for the participants?
• If you will have assigned seating, will you need table numbers?
• Will you need any of Dr. Comer's books or other SDP publications?
Room Arrangement
• Do you plan to set up the room the night before the event or have you made arrangements for someone to set up the room according to your specifications?
• Is the room comfortable for adult learners?
• Is the set-up conducive to group discussions and to listening to a speaker?
• Are you going to use round tables or rectangular tables? (We have found that 7–8 people at a table is optimal.)
• Will there be sign-in tables?

Question
Room Arrangement (continued)
• Will there be a table at the front for presentation materials?
• By what method will you assign participants to tables?
• Will the participants at each table represent a cross section of the audience?
• Will you put participants' table numbers on their nametags?
• Will you be serving refreshments?
• Do you need to set up the coffeepots the night before?
• Do you have tables for the refreshments?
• Will the tables be set up so as not to disturb the presentation?
• Who will monitor the refreshments?
• Will you remember to ask everyone to help clean up?
• Who will reassemble the meeting space after the training is over?
• If participants are to write on chart paper, is there enough space around the chart stands to accommodate them?
Final Details, Evaluations, and Assessment of Impact
• How will you assess whether the workshop achieved the desired outcomes?
• Who will summarize and prepare the evaluations?
• Do the evaluations need to be distributed? If so, to whom and how?
• Have all the bills been paid?
• Has all the paperwork been completed?
• Have you sent thank you letters with the summary of the evaluations to outside consultants?
• Have you considered what will be the follow-up to this workshop?
• How will you know that the workshop made a difference or had the intended impact on student learning and development?

Figure 7.7 Subcommittee activity assessment and future-planning form

Name of Subcommittee	Date
Name of Activity	

Question
• Did the result of this event/activity meet the preplanned objectives?
• How well did this activity support the goals of our Comprehensive School Plan?
• How well did this activity support each of the developmental pathways?
• How well did this activity support the Core Curriculum Content Standards?
• What went well?
• Were there any challenges or obstacles?
• What are some possible changes for next time?
• Did we have enough staff ownership of this activity?
• Did we have enough participation of the staff and parents?
• Did SPMT representatives go to their constituency groups to seek their support and participation well in advance of the event?
• Did adequate discussion occur with the SPMT?
• How could we generate even more ownership and participation next time?
• Was the event placed on the master calendar?
• Did we have a written plan that was distributed to staff that included timelines and responsibilities?
• Were our handouts relevant?
• Were overheads and handouts in appropriate languages?
• Did we ask participants to assess the event?
• What follow-up is now needed with staff?
• What follow-up is now needed with parents?
• What follow-up is now needed with students?

Figure 7.8 Subcommittee form

Name of school _____   District _____

Subcommittee name _____

Subcommittee members:

_____   _____

_____   _____

_____   _____

_____   _____

_____   _____

_____   _____

_____   _____

_____   _____

Chairperson: _____   Recorder: _____

Facilitator: _____   Timekeeper: _____

Do you have parent/family representatives serving on your committee?

Yes____ No____ If yes, please place an asterisk (*) by their name(s) above.

Please write the day, time, and place of subcommittee meetings:

Day _____   Time _____

Place _____

Please note:

1. The chairperson notifies your Comer facilitator whenever your regular meeting is not held.

2. The chairperson or recorder keeps a copy of all meeting agendas, minutes, attendance sheets, etc. Whenever the Comer facilitator is not present, a copy of these documents should be given to the Comer facilitator and the School Management Team/School Planning and Management Team (SMT/SPMT) recorder at the SMT/SPMT meetings. The Comer facilitator is responsible for submitting these documents to the Yale implementation coordinator or the district-level Comer director/supervisor monthly.

Goal(s):   _____

_____

_____

Objective(s):   _____

_____

_____

_____

_____

(Continued)

Figure 7.8   (Continued)

Tasks/Responsibilities: _____

_____

_____

_____

_____

_____

_____

_____

_____

_____

_____

_____

_____

_____

_____

_____

_____

_____

_____

_____

_____

_____

_____

SOURCE: Adapted from a form developed by V. Winters, Duffield Elementary School, Detroit Public Schools. It is used here courtesy of V. Winters and Duffield Elementary School.

Assessing Activities and Planning for Future Activities

Ongoing evaluation is essential to ongoing success in meeting the needs of the school community. After each activity or event—whether training and development or social—subcommittees should take the time to answer the questions that appear in Figure 7.7, "Subcommittee activity assessment and future-planning form."

Subcommittee Form

The subcommittee form (see Figure 7.8) should be completed at the beginning of the year. It is designed to be a road map for the work of the subcommittee, outlining goals, objectives, and tasks. It can be reviewed and modified throughout the year and should be shared with the SPMT as well as with the district level Comer director or supervisor.

Keeping Subcommittees at the Heart of the Process

As we have said time and again, SDP is not an add-on to something else you do in a school—nor are the subcommittees. Too often we have seen schools that organize the subcommittees and assign staff to every subcommittee but never even consider including parent members or students at the high school level. These subcommittees work hard all year, and yet there is no measurable difference in academic and social achievement in their schools. This often happens when subcommittees do not use the Comprehensive School Plan to drive their work or when they do not take the time to plan and assess activities using the developmental pathways as a framework or when they forget to consult the year-long school calendar. It also happens when more time, energy, and participation is placed on the social aspects of the Climate Subcommittee and only four or five members sign up for the CIA Subcommittee. It happens when subcommittees meet and never communicate with the SPMT or with the entire school population. We also see schools with too many subcommittees, draining staff energy from the most important task—effective teaching and learning in the classrooms.

Take the time in your schools to be thoughtful and strategic in planning and implementing your subcommittees. They are at the heart of the process. When sub-committees operate effectively, schools take pride in their work, and staff members have more energy to focus on curriculum, instruction, relationships, and development in their daily work—the bottom line of SDP.

8

Community Investment in Schools

Larry Dornell Burgess

When mutually beneficial relationships are established first, effective community partnerships flourish and endure. The principal of a Minneapolis elementary/middle school that welcomes 25 community volunteers each day describes his method of creating and supporting these relationships and partnerships and offers guidelines for "positive problem solving."

The Nellie Stone Johnson Community School in Minneapolis is the first school in Minnesota's history to be named after a living person. Nellie Stone Johnson was a neighborhood community advocate who passed away in March of 2002, and the community school that honors her was erected just prior to that in the fall of 2001. Community members wanted a school in their area that would meet their needs. They wanted a place for community gardening, after-school activities, and evening classes. They also wanted the school to be a place where they could come and support children during the day.

Our school is located in the Hawthorne community of North Minneapolis. The Hawthorne Huddle is a forum where the leaders in the community come together once a month, and they've invited the neighborhood schools to be a part of this. At one such forum, I spoke about some of the concerns I had as principal at our school.

Our school reflects the diversity of the neighborhood. Of our 725 pre-K through eighth-grade students, 60 percent are African American, 19 percent are Asian American, 18 percent are Latino, 3 percent are European American, and the remainder are Native American. In addition, poverty is high: 85 percent of our children are eligible for free or reduced lunch. At the Hawthorne Huddle, I talked about our students' reading, about field trips, and about ways the community could support our children. I was asked, "If you could get us to help you do one thing, what would it be?" I responded, "Come into our school and spend time with us first, then we can see what needs to be done and where you can help us most."

THE COMMUNITY-SCHOOL RELATIONSHIP WORKS BOTH WAYS

When I talk with people, I tell them that a community-school partnership is just like a relationship with a significant other. In order to make a successful partnership you must first come together. You need to spend time getting to know each other, and you have to get to know what each other's needs are, because we'll all receive from the relationship that we are creating. For these reasons, we did not begin our relationship with our potential partners by asking for any monetary things. This was not as important as our need for more adults in our building to help us meet the needs of our children. Once we allowed partners to come into our building and get to know what we were about, then they were in a position to say, "This is what we would like to help you with." They were able to talk with decision makers in various companies, who could then give us things that we were thinking about anyway.

We also are partnering with the University of Minnesota, which has allowed their psychologist and their social worker to come to work in our school with some of our neediest children. And we have partnerships with General Mills and Cargil, two locally based corporations. These partnerships provide us donations of time as well as money.

In other schools, corporate partnerships tend to fade very quickly. They have people from the corporate world who are initially very excited, but that excitement fades because they soon see that schools have more than one problem and those problems are tough. But we have learned that people stay enthusiastic when the children are involved. We have children sending artwork to the staff members of our corporate partners, who in turn put the artwork up in their offices. Some of them become pen pals with the children, using computer technology, e-mail, or just simple letter writing, to communicate on a regular basis. Certain staff people with these companies have "adopted" students, acting as mentors to them. After-school activities are also helpful because these are the times when school families and employees from the large companies come together.

COMMUNITY VOLUNTEERS AND THE SPMT

The school provides guidance through a curriculum/volunteer coordinator whose role it is to recruit and train volunteers. Before people can volunteer in schools they have to go through a background check and a qualifying process. We then have a volunteering session in which potential volunteers hear from one of my staff members about how they can get involved, whether it's in reading, homework, or just making phone calls.

There are so many things that people can do just to be a friend with someone else. It is not necessarily always giving in the traditional sense. For many students the greatest gift is just to be a friend. Just to be a big brother or big sister is sometimes all that children are looking for—to have someone to hear them during some of their most difficult times. Sometimes all the child needs is a response. We do our best to make sure the experience is a positive one for everyone. If a volunteer says, "I'm trying, but it doesn't seem to be working," or "I have a problem," we pair that individual with a person who has been volunteering for quite a while.

Volunteers and community members sit on our School Planning and Management Team (SPMT) and meet with us informally on a regular basis. We talk about how we can maximize the money we have in order to meet the needs of our children. We also talk about the curriculum. Our corporate partners have helped us develop the writing curriculum and the reading curriculum. Nurses from the University of Minnesota have delivered curricular units on asthma, personal hygiene, and proper relationships. People from Cargil and General Mills have trained teachers in computers and technology. And volunteers from Village Social Services created and taught sex education units to our middle school students.

Volunteers come into our building at all hours of the day; some come during their lunchtime. What I've noticed—and what makes me feel very good—is that some of them are coming just for 35 or 45 minutes. I see people sitting in corners reading to children or computing math problems. I see that they are talking with a child, and I think that this is rewarding not only for our children but also for the school and the volunteers.

Volunteers also come in after school to spend a few hours with our children because a lot of our parents cannot afford day care. Volunteers provide homework assistance until parents are able to leave their work and we can safely send the child home. On any given day, you might find 25 to 30 volunteers come in our building. It is a true illustration of putting the village to work in order to raise the child!

DOES YOUR SCHOOL MEET YOUR OWN CHILD'S NEEDS?

I live in the community and my daughter goes to my school, so I can speak very strongly about my belief in my school. And I say this to everybody: If you are a good administrator, if you are as good a teacher as you say you are, then you should entrust your own child to be in the environment that you are making.

9

Forging Strong Home, School, and Community Links

Michael Ben-Avie

For over 35 years, the School Development Program has promoted family involvement in education. As the following chapters will show, all members of the school community benefit when there are strong home, school, and community links.

Although many agree that effective parent and family involvement is crucial in supporting children's learning at school, many more are still unclear as to how to go about bridging the home and the school. For over 35 years, the School Development Program (SDP) has promoted family involvement in education. The underlying reasons for family involvement cannot be overstated: (1) Children have to see that their teachers respect their parents, and (2) children have to see that their parents respect their teachers. We have observed that when all the adults in children's lives pool their collective wisdom and collaborate, then a seamless web of authority emerges that supports children's learning and development.

Family involvement can occur at different levels of time and commitment. For some parents, involvement means attendance at parent-teacher conferences, support of school events, and the monitoring of their children's homework and school progress. Other parents volunteer daily in the school. Still others are official and permanent members of the school's SPMT, the central planning body within the school.

One way to think about parents as partners in education is to distinguish between at-school involvement and at-home involvement. SDP stands for the promotion of both types of family involvement.

AT-SCHOOL FAMILY INVOLVEMENT

When parents are involved at school, they welcome visitors to the school, mentor students, volunteer in the classroom or cafeteria, accompany students on field trips, talk with students about their jobs, and assist teachers. In many SDP schools, parents set up a family center in the school. The family center at Eugenio Maria de Hostos Microsociety School in Yonkers, for example, is a large room near the main office of the school. In the center are couches, computers, telephones, a fax machine, and books and materials for parents to read. Parents entering the center are greeted by other parents with a cup of coffee and a little something to eat. Parents organize computer lessons for other parents as well as health campaigns. Parents learn from one another about how to handle certain situations with their children and how to navigate the variety of social service agencies.

AT-HOME FAMILY INVOLVEMENT

At-home involvement with young children includes practicing with them the type of talking that goes on in classrooms, which helps them become prepared for school. When engaging in classroom talk, the child knows that you know the answer to the question being asked. What are the days of the week? Why is it not a good idea to shake a bottle of soda? In classroom talk, careful attention is paid to turn-taking and waiting patiently while another speaks. This is an important skill that can be practiced at home.

Another kind of talking is a running narrative of what you are doing: "I am going to take a step backwards before I put the french fries in the hot oil because I want to make sure that the hot oil doesn't splash me." Even if the child does not ask any questions, learning is going on. Parents can also help their children name feelings: "It sounds to me from what you're saying that you were *disappointed* you couldn't go to your friend's house." Especially helpful with older children is providing counter examples to some of their statements: "Does *everybody* really hate you? Can you think of someone who doesn't hate you? Is there one part of your body that you do think is attractive?" At-home engagement in education especially includes helping children think through experiences that they have had at school and in other settings.

PARENT-TEACHER COLLABORATIONS

We have learned the importance of a formal home-school-community program—one that involves teachers as well as parents. Just as parents might not know how to navigate in the school setting, teachers might not know how to engage parents in the school. For example, teachers are not taught as part of their training how to talk to parents. I recall that every day when I would pick up my son from preschool, the teacher would report to me all the trouble my son had gotten into during the day. I began to dread walking into the school. One day I asked the teacher whether my son had done anything good. Gradually, I taught her how to talk to me as a parent.

Involving families in education cannot be left up to the individual initiative of a teacher or parent. In schools where we have seen meaningful parent engagement, the Parent Team has worked out with the principal and the teams the ways that it can meaningfully support the learning and development of all the children in the school. Moreover, since collaborative relationships based on mutual trust and respect were established between the school and the home, the schools worked with the parents to find ways to support them. The take-home message of the following chapter on family involvement is that all the adults in the school community benefit when there are strong home-school-community links.

FROM ONE PARENT TO ANOTHER

As parents ourselves, we have had our fair share of looking at our children and wondering whether we are doing a good job raising them. There are moments when we observe them and we are touched by how much they have learned and developed. There are other times, however, when it seems that the only reason we had children was in order to wrench our emotions. How can it be, we wonder, that the same children whose maturity and brightness impressed us so much yesterday could today break the flower pot while fighting? We remember moments when we felt discouraged and our children sensed that we needed a smile and a few quiet minutes. As parents, we don't have to be perfect. What's important is that at the end of the road, our grown-up children will turn to us and say, "You weren't so bad as a parent." And at that moment, we can explain how, specifically, we promoted their learning and development.

10

Families
as Partners

Parent Teams and Parent/Family Involvement

Sheila Jackson, Nora Martin, and Jan Stocklinski

The term parent/family involvement *refers to all the different ways that parents and other family members can support their children. Whether occurring at home or in school, this support has a direct impact on students' academic and social achievement. (Note that "family members" may be biological relatives or other individuals who have some or total legal responsibility for a student's well-being and school success.) The home-school partnership is* not *an event or a series of events; it is not a numbers game. Rather, the partnership is a process of building relationships that provide support to the children and adolescents in school so that all children achieve well in and out of school. This chapter presents detailed and comprehensive guidelines, checklists, and activities to ensure the fullest participation of parents and families.*

Over the last 15-plus years we have provided professional development to parent teams throughout the schools in Prince George's County, Maryland, Detroit, Michigan, and numerous other school systems. Sheila Jackson is supervisor and human resources team leader, Comer Office and the School Development Program (SDP) Regional Training Center, Prince George's County Public Schools. Nora Martin is a professor at the College of Education, Eastern

Michigan University (EMU), and a codirector of regional SDP training conducted jointly by EMU and the Detroit Public Schools. Jan Stocklinski is a senior implementation coordinator at SDP.

Our work has given us insight into effective ways to involve families in schools. We have learned not to talk about "parent involvement" but rather "parent/family involvement." This is, in part, because *parent* is limiting in definition, particularly in the very diverse world in which we now live. We now have one-parent families, two-parent families, extended families, adopted families, grandparents-raising-children families, homeless families, and many more. Our experiences have taught us that the language we use may send unintended messages.

In this chapter, we are not focusing on work that is done directly with parents and families. Rather, we are focusing on SDP's work with the school-based Parent Team and that team's role in involving parents and families at all levels of school life. We focus on the process of building a program and on creating solutions based on self-diagnosed needs. Our strategy in this chapter is to draw attention to the key steps and principles involved in building a program for parents and families and to provide a few templates to guide team discussions, as well as sample exercises and resource lists of program ideas for further development and adaptation to your site.

The intent of a formal program for parents and families is to establish a home-school partnership. It serves to reduce the cultural gap that may exist between the home and school, thereby fostering a climate of partnership. SDP enables school personnel and parents/families who may be alienated from one another (for whatever reasons) to begin working together on neutral tasks rather than to start with complex—perhaps even value-laden—issues. By working together on specific events, school personnel and parents/families can begin getting to know one another, learn to respect one another, and eventually view themselves as participants in a collaborative enterprise rather than as adversaries in a competitive power play.

INSIGHTS INTO THE HOME-SCHOOL PARTNERSHIP

Parent/family involvement is a key element of SDP. SDP recognizes the critical role parents can and should play in their children's education from the moment they first enter the schoolhouse to graduation day.

With care and nurturing, an emotional attachment and bond develops between the child, the parents, and the family. This bond allows the family to influence the child's development along the critical developmental pathways necessary for learning and growing well in today's society. Through day-to-day life with their families, children learn all kinds of things. For example, when a curious child asks questions and receives answers and explanations from parents or other significant adult members of the family, those adults are stimulating and encouraging that child's development. When the adults show that they are interested in reading, the child internalizes the idea of reading as something important. The motivation for learning, therefore, grows out of the child's relationship (attachment and bonding) with important and valued adults.

A child from a "nonmainstream," marginal family is likely to have missed out on such early stimulation and enters school unprepared to meet the expectations of school, a mainstream institution. A child is expected to learn to read at school, but may come from a home in which no one reads and may never have heard a parent read bedtime stories. The child's language skills may be "underdeveloped" or "nonstandard." There are other areas in which expectations at home and at school may be radically at odds. For example, in some families a child who does not fight back will be punished. A child then goes to school and gets in trouble when he or she fights back. For children who come to school "underdeveloped" or "differently developed," school becomes even more challenging by second and third grades, and by eight or nine years of age children have developed the cognitive capacity to understand why they and their family are different from the people at school.

Parents/families are the source of a child's self-affirmation. Children will believe what the people they love and trust believe, including how they feel about school. If parents mistrust the school and staff, their children will more than likely feel the same way and may feel alienated from school and staff. In order to overcome that mistrust, parents/families must be made to feel comfortable and welcome in the school. Only then can they work effectively with school staff in support of all aspects of the child's development. It is important for schools to learn how to create a welcoming and comfortable environment and to constantly examine what things the school does (unconsciously or consciously) that make parents/families feel shut out. Too often (mostly unconsciously) the barriers to parent/family involvement are found within school practices and policies. Exploring these barriers should be one of the first tasks of the Parent Team, as we will discuss later in this chapter.

In summary, the relationships between parents/families and school personnel are central to the establishment of a positive school climate that supports the healthy development of children.

CATEGORIES OF PARENT/FAMILY INVOLVEMENT

The parent program is best conceptualized as a multilevel process with three distinct yet overlapping participatory categories: broad participation and support, active daily participation in schools, and participation in school management.

Broad Participation and Support

The first and broadest type of involvement encompasses the many general ways in which parents and families support their children's education, both at home and at school. The act of sending children to school ready for school is parental involvement; so is the act of insisting that the children work hard, respect others, and complete their homework. Reading to children, involving them in activities outside of school, cooking and shopping with them—all these constitute parental involvement in education. Families may be involved at school through membership in the home-school organization (called PTA, PTSA, PTO, Parent Advisory Group) and/or through attending or contributing to various school activities such as potluck dinners, school performances, parades, open house events, home-school organization meetings, report card conferences, sports events, bake sales, family fun days, and picnics.

General events that encourage and permit broad-based family participation serve several important purposes. They create opportunities to meet the needs outlined in the Comprehensive School Plan for parents and families. Consider what can be accomplished at family math nights or at workshops offered for families on such topics as communication skills for parents and staff, state testing and what it means at home, problem solving strategies around issues families face, or how to create science fair projects. At the same time, well-thought-out activities such as these can break down barriers between parents/families and school staff. By working together on projects, families and staff can see each other as adults with common goals. This can help create a school climate that is inviting, caring, and accepting.

Active Participation in Schools

Parent/family involvement is raised to another level when family members become engaged in the day-to-day life of the school in such activities as

- volunteering in classrooms, the office, the cafeteria, or the library
- chaperoning field trips or before- or afterschool activities
- tutoring children before, during, or after school
- taking "welcoming" duty before or after school or participating in "parent patrols"

In this category, parents/families are in the building taking part in the school's educational programs—they are learning and growing along with students and staff. Children see their family members interacting with school personnel and are more likely to imitate, identify with, and internalize the values and goals of the school.

Participation in School Management

At the third and highest level of involvement, parents participate as decision-makers in school governance and management. They may play a leadership role in the parent organization, serve on the School Planning and Management Team (SPMT) or on one of the subcommittees, speak before the board of education on behalf of the Parent Team, or contribute to school staff or parent group development. By participating at this level, parents develop the social, organizational, and political skills needed to bring about institutional change. They also become more involved in understanding school data and may participate in writing the school plan. The hoped-for result is that more parent/family activities will truly reflect the goals of the plan and make a difference for all the students in a particular community.

Schools need to appreciate and acknowledge that parent/family involvement is very complex and is a matter of building relationships over time. Understanding the value and purpose of all three types of parental involvement and what can be achieved with each is a critical first step in establishing a parent program. In the most developed parent programs, family and parent involvement will be seen in all three categories.

STEPS TO BUILDING THE HOME-SCHOOL PARTNERSHIP

There are three basic steps in building parent/family involvement in SDP schools: understanding parent/family involvement at your school, forming the Parent Team

Figure 10.1 Ten truths of parent/family involvement

1. All parents have hopes and goals for their children.

   They differ in how they support their children's efforts to achieve those goals.

2. The home is one of several spheres of influence that simultaneously shape a child.

   The school must work in concert with other spheres for the child's benefit, not push them apart.

3. The parent is the central contributor to a child's education.

   Schools can either co-opt that role or recognize the potential of the parent.

4. Parent involvement must be a legitimate element of education.

   It deserves equal emphasis with elements such as program improvement and evaluation.

5. Parent involvement is a process, not a program of activities.

   It requires ongoing energy and effort.

6. Parents' interaction with their own children is the cornerstone of parent involvement.

   A program must recognize the value, diversity, and difficulty of this role.

7. Parent involvement requires a vision, policy, and framework.

   A consensus of understanding is important.

8. Most barriers to parent involvement are found within school practices.

   They are not found within parents.

9. Any parent can be "hard to reach."

   Parents must be identified and approached individually; they are not defined by gender, ethnicity, family situation, education, or income.

10. Successful parent involvement nurtures relationships and partnerships.

    It strengthens the bonds between home and school, parent and educator, parent and child, school and community.

SOURCE: Courtesy of RMC Research Corporation, Portsmouth, New Hampshire.

and building parent/family membership on committees, and examining barriers to parent/family involvement and working out solutions.

Understanding Parent/Family Involvement at Your School

One of the first steps to working on increasing parent/family involvement is to understand the different levels of involvement as described above. Another step is to assess and appreciate what is already in place. The staff and active parents and family members should discuss why they want more involvement and what the term *more involvement* means to them. This in itself takes some understanding, much dialogue, and consensus building.

In building awareness of factors in parental involvement, it is important for staff to examine their attitudes, values, and feelings relative to the students they teach and their families. We have found that without a positive belief system in the families and students we serve, parent/family involvement will not flourish. The "Ten truths of parent/family involvement" (Figure 10.1) would be good material for such discussions. Families and school staff need to read these as starters and dialogue about them. "Let's react to some of these statements. How do you feel about them? Do you

Figure 10.2 Understanding parent/family involvement at your school

1. Identify all the parents and/or family members who are involved as individuals or in groups in your building.

2. Clarify the functions and activities of each group:
    • Which parents/families does each group target and reach? Discuss discrepancies if any.
    • Which group will be the official Parent Team?
    • Is a PTA/PTO/PTSA already in place?
    • Will this be the Parent Team?
    • Will changes have to be made to ensure that this team is representative of your student population?

3. Determine what your school staff mean when they say, "We want more parent/family involvement." Once this is done:
    • What needs to be done to increase the level of involvement?
    • How does this fit into your Comprehensive School Plan?

4. Does your school provide a warm and welcoming environment for parents and families? If not:
    • What needs to be done?
    • Which teams or subcommittees will work on this?
    • How does this fit into your Comprehensive School Plan?

5. Does your school already have a good system for regular communication? If not:
    • How, specifically, can the Parent Team communicate regularly with its constituency groups?
    • How, specifically, can the entire staff work on regular communication?

believe that _____ is true?" It is important to have a skilled facilitator lead the discussions to make the process helpful and constructive for the school.

Figure 10.2 displays the initial questions to be addressed in planning for parent involvement. Building consensus around parent involvement is easier to accomplish when the school staff is already working fairly well together and operating from an existing plan. A vision of what parent involvement will be at your school should evolve from the discussions and should then be incorporated into the Comprehensive School Plan.

Forming the Parent Team and Building Family Membership on Subcommittees

Formation of the Parent Team is a critical step. The Parent Team, which is one of the three major teams of the Comer Process, can be your already existing PTA, PTO, PTSA, PTF, if that team is willing to fulfill the responsibilities of the Parent Team as outlined in Figure 10.3. The SPMT and existing parent organization need to discuss the following questions:

Figure 10.3 Responsibilities of the parent team

- Plans and coordinates activities that support the goals identified in the Comprehensive School Plan
- Ensures that all dates and activities planned by the team are compatible with the overall school calendar
- Addresses the needs of the larger parent/family community
- Communicates with the SPMT (Family members serve on the SPMT and on all subcommittees.)
- Uncovers barriers to parent/family involvement and develops strategies to overcome the barriers, working collaboratively with the SPMT and Parent/Family Involvement Subcommittee (if this subcommittee exists)

- Is the present team representative of our parent/family community? Or if we worked differently, could it be?
- Does it represent the different geographic areas our families come from?
- Does it represent ethnic, racial, and cultural groups in our school?
- Does it represent a cross-section of grade levels?
- Is the team willing to carry out the responsibilities of the Parent Team as outlined for SDP schools?

Once the Parent Team is operational, it works hand in hand with the SPMT and subcommittees to carry out the goals of the Comprehensive School Plan.

In addition, all the subcommittees in a school should seek parent/family membership on their committees by assessing the interests and needs of the larger parent community. This naturally depends on what skills and strengths parents/families bring to the school and are willing to develop with support from school staff. The staff needs to reach out in a strong, personal, and sincere way to recruit family members to serve on committees. In addition, ongoing and regular team-building work on the committees will be necessary to create the sort of climate that makes parents and staff alike want to continue on the team—that makes everyone feel that their contributions are worthwhile. We offer some suggestions for team-building activities in the section on Staff-Parent Training later in this chapter.

Examining Barriers to Parent/Family Involvement and Working Out Solutions

Once the Parent Team is formed, a major challenge will be to uncover the reasons parents or families are not as involved as is necessary to make a difference academically and socially for all the students in your school. This is best accomplished by using a problem-solving strategy to discover the barriers and to brainstorm for solutions that will work for your school and community. We suggest that the team start by identifying what is working and then move to problem solving the barriers, and we offer guides for this exercise in Figures 10.4 and 10.5. There are many problem-solving formats; Figure 10.5 offers just one example. Many schools, families, and staff have used this process.

While we encourage you to diagnose your own barriers and work toward solutions, as an additional resource we have compiled in Figures 10.6 and 10.7 a list of some of the challenges that others have faced and possible solutions. The list is divided into staff barriers and parent/family barriers. What is important to consider is that parent/family involvement is enhanced when the staff's commitment is as strong as that of the parents and families.

STAFF-PARENT TRAINING FOR PARENT/FAMILY INVOLVEMENT

When a school begins the SDP process, parents and staff alike must be trained in the overall concepts and the role of the Parent Team, SPMT, subcommittees, and comprehensive school planning. This is an ongoing process that must continue from year to year as new parents and staff come to the school. Depending on the topic and the need, sometimes it may be preferable to train parents and families by themselves. At other times, it is ideal to have parents and staff train together. Not only do the groups learn the content at the same time, but also they have the opportunity to build relationships and get to know one another in a setting in which their roles are equalized. Parents should also serve on the Adult Development and Training Subcommittee in the school in order to help plan training. We have found that it is quite powerful when parents and staff begin to cotrain together, finding new opportunities to build relationships.

Figures 10.8 and 10.9 are sample materials that we have found particularly effective for team building and for stimulating discussion at the introductory phases of parent/family involvement work.

- Figure 10.8 is an example of a people search. At every event involving staff and parents, include a team-builder activity that connects to the event and encourages participants to really get to know each other. It is often easier to come back to school when you know others who will be there. Encourage the staff to reach out to meet and mingle with families.

- Figure 10.9 is a discussion activity entitled "Headbands" (Perrin, 1985) that we call "Hats." This activity allows participants to experience and observe the effect of attitude and communication on staff/parent/family involvement. "Headbands" is found in Kate Perrin's (1985) *National Leadership Camp: Leadership Curriculum Guide* (pp. 8–10).

PROMISING PRACTICES AND PROGRAMS

Figure 10.10 brings together the critical practices that we have found important in parent and family involvement. We invite you to read through these to evaluate which concepts are already in place in your school and which practices could be

Figure 10.4 Examining parent/family involvement practices

List **three or more promising practices** and **three or more promising programs** (in your experience) that have proven to be highly successful in improving parent/family involvement.

1.

2.

3.

4.

5.

6.

List the **three major obstacles/deterrents** to the improvement of parent/family involvement in your school/district.

1.

2.

3.

Develop **at least one strategy** to overcome each obstacle/deterrent you have identified.

1.

2.

3.

Choose one of the above to implement in your school.

Figure 10.5   A problem-solving technique

"Avoid that tug of war. . . . Guide your team through structured positive problem solving."

Step 1 <u>Think</u> about one challenge you face regarding parent/family involvement.

Step 2 <u>Pair</u> with one person at your table. <u>Discuss</u> each challenge/problem.

Step 3 <u>Share</u> at your table. <u>Decide</u> on one challenge/problem to take through a structured problem-solving session.

Step 4 <u>Write</u> your challenge/problem on chart paper as a "how to" statement.

Step 5 <u>Brainstorm</u> and <u>record</u> possible solutions as "I wish" statements.

Step 6 <u>Read</u> your list, <u>clarify</u>, and <u>combine</u> statements.

Step 7 <u>Distribute</u> dots (maybe 10 to each person). Have each person <u>mark</u> his or her three top choices with dots. (If you feel strongly about one idea, you could even put 8 of your dots next to that one and one dot on another idea and one dot on a third idea.) The intent is to weigh your choices.

Step 8 <u>Find</u> a partner whose view may differ from yours. Together <u>decide</u> on one top choice between the two of you. <u>Go</u> to the chart paper together and place another larger dot (or different color dot) on your choice.

Step 9 Have the entire group <u>look</u> at the list and ask them if any <u>clarification</u> is <u>needed</u>.

Step 10 <u>Combine</u> any solutions that are similar. <u>Check</u> with the persons who put them up to see if they agree to the combination.

Step 11 As a group, <u>look for patterns</u>. <u>Narrow your choices</u>. You are looking for where the most <u>energy</u> is for making a change.

Step 12 <u>Make a decision</u>. Pick a solution based on all the data.

SOURCE: Based on the work of "Problem-Solving for Practical Innovation" developed by Charlene Pasco, Ph.D. (1988). Courtesy of Prince George's County Public Schools, Maryland.

added or expanded. Dialogue about these concepts is an excellent beginning for the Parent Team, SPMT, or the climate subcommittee, as well as a subject for discussion at general faculty and grade-level meetings.

Your practices should guide you as you institute programs that will enhance the goals and objectives of the Comprehensive School Plan. There are hundreds and hundreds of programs and strategies that have been used at every level to bring about greater parent/family involvement and support in schools. As a resource, we have compiled specific ideas that others have found useful in Figure 10.11, "Strategies to increase home-school cooperation."

These lists cover a great deal of material. You may be thinking, "Where do we start?" There is no cookie cutter approach to parent/family involvement. There are, however, some basic steps, which we have included earlier. We urge you to first assess what you have in place and what is already working. Time and time again people say to us that they have poor parent/family involvement, yet when we work with the school we find many successful programs and practices in place. So start where you are and build on those strengths. Think attitude first: What are the attitudes of staff and parents relative to parents and families? From there, use the processes and committees in place to create the optimal situation.

(Text continues on page 125)

Figure 10.6   Overcoming staff barriers to the home-school partnership

Staff Barriers
1. Lack of common understanding about the definition of the home-school partnership • Develop a common definition of the home-school partnership across the school community that includes appreciating parents we might not ever physically see but who: call and ask questions support the school and teacher verbally at home read to their children and work with them at home provide concrete experiences for their children outside of the school • As a staff, establish specific tasks and activities for which parent/family involvement and participation is needed; publicize these early and often.
2. Resistance by staff to having parents/families involved in school in any way • Understand that it is difficult for all human beings to learn to share power. When those first difficult attempts at power sharing are made, commend the initiative and point out specifically how this collaboration is enhancing the overall effort toward improving the school. • Take staff on a tour of the attendance area as a way of helping them to feel comfortable with the community. • Historically, staff may have felt parents' lack of trust or reluctance to communicate. In the past, many parents have had no contact with the staff members except to receive bad news, such as a child's academic or behavioral failures. Encourage staff to contact parents regularly with good news about their children.
3. Unwillingness to make the necessary investment of time • Help staff to understand how home-school partnerships around academic and psychosocial development goals can make their classroom tasks easier. • Ask staff to divide up the calendar of scheduled events and take turns attending. • Help staff understand that the idea of partnerships with parents is not only about attending meetings and events, but rather, it is about developing relationships based upon mutual respect and shared responsibility for teaching children well. • Encourage social events for families and staff that (1) emphasize interaction and relaxation and de-emphasize roles (such as potluck suppers and musical programs), and (2) are tied into your school goals for academic growth and positive climate development.
4. Lack of time available in the existing schedule • Initially honor and work within the time constraints of the staff. • Collaboratively problem solve to decide times that honor the time constraints of staff as well as parents.
5. No built-in welcoming and/or reaching out when parents enter school • Train entire staff to greet and welcome parents/families wherever they are in the building. Include support staff in training to welcome and invite parents/families. • Make sure that the school physically reflects the language and culture of all students in artwork, signage, etc. • Make sure that the building and grounds are clean and inviting. • Create a "welcome wagon" packet or program to welcome new and entering parents/families and provide them with basic information to support a comfortable transition into school.

(Continued)

Figure 10.6 (Continued)

---

6. Lack of skills/knowledge in how to work with all parents/families

- Create a climate in which all staff are comfortable in admitting this.

- Have training for staff in how to effectively hold parent/teacher conferences as well as how to present in front of adults.

- Urge teacher-training institutions to build in more preservice training on effective parent/family involvement strategies.

7. Communications that are too boring, complicated, long, or negative

- Hold staff workshops on effective positive communication skills for verbal and written communication as well as for effective outreach strategies.

- Provide training to improve the telephone skills of everyone in the front office.

- Shorten communications.

- Make sure that communications are bilingual as needed.

- Discuss all items to be sent home via students in class with the students.

- Send positive communications home, not just negative notes or problems.

- Make personal contacts as often as possible—not just written notes.

- Use creative methods for children to tell their parents that there is a meeting at school: Have children write invitations with a space for RSVP signatures; stamp a figure or smiling face on child's hand to remind parents of an evening meeting; make a string necklace designed in the shape of a house or animal and attach to meeting notice information.

- Remember to multitask whenever you see parents/families—use every moment to connect about upcoming activities/events.

- Consider making home visits from time to time. Invite a few families to a coffee hour with the principal at the home of another parent/family.

8. Lack of understanding of "culture" of families (system for living)

- Train staff in developing school practices that accommodate the growing diversity of the families they serve.

- Recognize that a set of rules or expectations at home may be different from those at school. Bridge those differences without making students feel that what goes on at home is bad.

- Train staff to understand, recognize, and celebrate the multiple cultures, ethnicities, languages, and religions represented at the school.

- Allow students to work cooperatively.

- Have kids interview their families about their lives and culture.

- Establish a classroom speaker's bureau with parents/families so they can share their experiences, culture, hobbies, etc.

Figure 10.7 Overcoming parent and family member barriers to partnerships with school and district staff

Parent/Family Barriers
1. Psychological issues: fear, anxiety, school phobia, intimidation, etc.   • Work to develop staff sensitivity about one of the most significant obstacles in their communication with parents/families: the fact that many parents see themselves as educationally unqualified to be sharing decision making with college- and university-educated professional staff.   • Teach staff to model respect for all types of families.   • Recognize that all families want the best for their children.   • Make sure that all areas of the school are welcoming, inviting, and family-friendly and that all staff are trained to welcome and engage parents/families.   • Nurture positive relationships by socializing and teambuilding with parents at every meeting.   • Have nametags at all meetings.   • At every meeting make sure that staff mingle with, meet, greet, and sit with parents/families and do not cluster into a "staff choir."   • Invite experienced parents/families to share information about effective parent/teacher conferencing as well as knowledge and skills in how to work with teachers, the school, and the school system.   • Have teachers become more visible in the neighborhood.   • Establish a welcome wagon program for families new to the school.   • Call parents/families with good news before they contact you.   • Listen twice as much as we talk.   • Make invitations real and sincere. Avoid "surface only" invitations.
2. Prior negative experiences (as a student or as a parent in other schools)   • Build trust by listening to parents, inviting their input, and pairing them with individual staff members or other positively involved parents/families.   • Call parents with positive reports about their children.   • Provide students with recognition and rewards for academic achievement and positive social behavior to motivate and encourage them.   • Involve parents in planning social events.   • Hire staff that reflect the diversity of the students and the community.
3. Attention focused on basic survival needs   • Provide a warm, caring, and no-fault climate for families under stress.   • Adjust the school's rules or program to accommodate difficult family circumstances.   • Make arrangements for parents who may have difficult schedules (due to family obligations, working several jobs, working unusual shifts) to be involved in school projects and activities.   • Arrange for transportation and child care for school events.   • Inform parents of services available to them in the community.   • Intervene in other institutions on behalf of parents and families.   • Create a dedicated "parent/family resource area" in the school.   • Provide refreshments or small meals for meetings.   • Assess socioeconomic impact of scheduled events: Can our families afford the admission to our events or the expense of participating in book fairs, bake sales, etc.?

(Continued)

Figure 10.7 (Continued)

---

4. Activities not meeting the needs of parents (no ties to school improvement plan and overall student-centered planning process)

- Make sure that parents are represented on all subcommittees and have an active role in developing, implementing, monitoring, and assessing the school improvement plan.
- Survey parents to find out what they like/dislike about the school as well as ways in which they would like to be involved. Assess their strengths and talents.
- In each monthly newsletter, publish names and phone numbers of parents/families who are willing to talk with other parents/families about concerns and interests.
- Make sure that the Parent Team is an ongoing problem-solving team by providing training sessions in creative problem solving and student-centered decision making.
- Be thoughtful about times and dates of meetings (make sure that meetings/events are not scheduled around holidays, tests, etc.).
- Make sure every meeting has a specific purpose—don't schedule meetings just to have meetings. Instead, make sure that all activities enhance student academic achievement and support psychosocial growth and development.
- Couple business meetings with student performances or exhibits.

---

5. Transportation

- Arrange transportation to and from meetings/events.
- Work with system and central office to allow parents to ride the bus with their child for specific activities.
- Move some meetings/conferences to community sites, e.g., malls, libraries, recreation centers.

---

6. Creating balance between male and female parent involvement

- Look for gender balance on teams and subcommittees, as well as for special events such as speakers on career day or assistants on field day.
- Always address notes home to males as well as females—if parents are living apart, send a separate note to each one.
- In scheduling home visits, find a time when both parents can be available.
- Invite "significant males" in the life of each student to become involved in some specific activity.
- Encourage adult males to chaperone field trips and lead classroom activities.
- Use inclusive language for volunteer positions ("room parent") as opposed to using traditional gender specific language such as "room mothers."
- Use inclusive language to embrace diverse family configurations—instead of "mother's day" and "father's day," use terms like "family day" or "my male/female role model/significant other day" or "my special person day."
- Refrain from judgment about families in which a child lives with only one parent or other family members.

---

7. Language

- Have staff learn the languages of the families with whom they interact.
- Have interpreters available for every meeting.

Figure 10.8   People search

The activity below is a sample of a People search. The format can be modified for many different purposes and settings. At every event involving staff and parents, include a team builder that connects to the event and encourages participants to really get to know each other. It is often easier to come back to school when you know others who will be there. Encourage the staff not to sit together, but to reach out to meet and greet families.	
Find and write the name of someone who . . .	**. . . fills the following description:**
	. . . has been a room parent for his/her own child or has actively recruited room parents for his/her classroom.
	. . . has served on a PTA/PTSA/PTO/Parent Team.
	. . . has walked into a school office and been ignored.
	. . . has been offended by what was said about his/her child at a parent conference.
	. . . holds regular evening meetings with the families of their students. (These meetings are different from regular PTA.) Share how it was done.
	. . . is a teacher or parent who attends most of the PTA meetings at the school where he/she teaches.
	. . . has found meaningful ways to engage the families of students in school. (Explain.)
	. . . meets and greets parents/families in the morning when they drop off their children.
	. . . refrains from becoming defensive when parents/staff/students come in angry or upset.
	. . . has four or more children of his/her own (or children in three different schools).
	. . . always looks for the strengths of families and children.
	. . . accepts and respects families and/or school staff who are different from themselves in some way.
	. . . calls home/school with positive messages during the year.

Figure 10.9   Headbands or Hats

This activity is used in the parental/family involvement training module to make specific points about the effect of attitude and communication on staff/parent/family involvement.

1. Presenter prepares headbands by writing a phrase on each one. Use lettering large enough to be seen by all members of the audience. The phrases can be modified or expanded based on local needs. Some examples are:

    - Laugh at me.

    - Speak only Spanish to me.

    - Smile at me, but do not mean it.

    - Turn your chairs away from me.

    - Treat me as the parent leader.

    - Seek my opinion.

    - Listen very carefully to me.

    - Look at my feet when you speak to me.

    - Disrespect all my ideas.

2. Presenter puts headbands on volunteers, making sure that they do not see the phrase on their own hat and asking observers not to yell out the phrases.

3. Ask everyone who is not in the circle of volunteers to be an observer.

4. The volunteer group discusses a designated topic, for example, "What is ideal parent and/or family involvement?"

5. Encourage each volunteer to speak at least several times.

6. Time them (7 minutes). Then applaud and thank them.

7. At the end, the presenter addresses each volunteer one by one, asking the volunteer to guess what is written on his or her own headband before the volunteer takes it off and reads the phrase.

8. The presenter gives all volunteers a chance to give their reactions about what they were feeling during the discussion in Steps 4–6.

9. The presenter asks them to make any connections and observations related to parent/family involvement.

10. After the volunteers comment, invite additional observations from the audience.

SOURCE: Adapted from Perrin (1985), © National Association of Secondary School Principals. Used with permission.

Figure 10.10 Promising practices for involving parents and families

Building Relationships
• Build relationships with parents, families, and students. Build on the strengths that families bring to school. Respect all families and parents, however they come to you.
• Make all parents, families, staff, and students feel welcome in the school.
• Know your community and identify its needs.
• Make sure representative parents serve on the SPMT and all subcommittees.
• Use a liaison to help make contacts with the community.
Adapting Events to Community Needs
• Schedule meetings around the needs of the community and vary your times.
• Schedule meetings around the master calendar of the school and the larger community.
• Schedule meetings with substance that reflect the needs of the Comprehensive School Plan and that meet the needs of the community.
• Obtain speakers who are role models for the community. Bring back graduates, etc.
• Conduct bilingual meetings and training if appropriate. Send out written notices in different languages. Send positive notes and make positive calls.
• Involve the students in the planned activities so they encourage their parents/families to become involved. Students can write invitations to their parents/families.
• Arrange special transportation if needed.
• At meetings, have nametags and sign-ins and have other parents, students, and staff serve as greeters at every meeting.
• Provide babysitting. (Use older children and an adult, Girl Scout-type groups, staff members, etc.)
• Start and end on time, taking no more than 1 1/2 hours.
• Always include icebreakers. Split into different groups so everyone gets to know each other. Ask staff to sit in different places—not all together—and ask them to reach out and greet parents and families. Modeling matters.
• Provide refreshments or snacks.
• When holding big community school activities (carnivals, dinners, socials, and multicultural activities), intentionally build relationships and connect the activity to the needs identified in the Comprehensive School Plan.
Appreciating Parents and Families
• Send appreciation notes home to parents and families who help with school projects. Consider a thank you luncheon for volunteers.
• Let parents and families know that they make a big difference. Make them feel that they are wanted and needed. Model positive behaviors. Be genuine in your relationships. Remember that there are real invitations and there are surface invitations.
• Ask staff to identify one or two families that they know well to come into school to share what they think is going well, what is not going well, and what may need to be changed.

• Appreciate parent/family involvement that includes the following:
 	
    A parent calling and asking questions
    A parent supporting the schools and teacher verbally at home
    Parents working with their children at home
    Parents reading to their children
    Parents providing concrete experiences for their children

Figure 10.11 Strategies to increase home-school cooperation

These ideas have come from many places, including Columbus, OH, San Diego, CA, Prince George's County, MD, and from teachers and parents throughout the SDP network. We encourage you to go through your own process of identifying the barriers and challenges at your school, and brainstorm for solutions that your school community will support. Additionally, all activities and events need to be based on the Comprehensive School Plan and tied as much as possible to curriculum, instruction, relationships, and development.

Relationship-Building Strategies

- Invite a few key parents/families to a coffee hour with the principal and hold it at the home of the PTSA/PTO/Parent Team leader.

- Invite several parents to sample the school lunch once a month. Seat them with the principal, teachers, and several randomly selected students.

- Provide an opportunity for parents to get together with other parents to discuss school problems.

- Encourage parents to meet with other parents to discuss school issues and then feed that discussion back through the Parent Team to the appropriate school team and/or committee.

- Consider home visits—if not to the home, then to community centers. Be visible in the community. Make families feel that you like being in the community and working with them.

- Set up a plan for the principal to make "house calls."

- Make sure your SSST is inviting and friendly to parents/families/students.

Communication and Information-Sharing Strategies

- Working with the Parent Team, create a "How Parents Can Help" handbook that gives practical suggestions and/or home activities such as making out grocery lists, taking nature walks, cooking and shopping together, planning and taking trips, helping to pay the bill at restaurants, etc.

- Send home "happy grams" and other good news notes about accomplishments and achievements.

- Establish a communication hotline for parents/guardians to check on nightly assignments and any events/activities.

- Hold high school department seminars for parents/guardians to help them help their children get the most out of particular course offerings.

- Establish regular visitation days for observation of classes and a chance for families to offer constructive suggestions.

- In each month's newsletter, publish the names and phone numbers of parents serving on teams and committees so other parents may contact them with ideas of interest or concern.

- Suggest an evening a week when parents or students can telephone the principal at school to ask questions and discuss problems.

- Encourage parents/families to praise their child's successes.

- Occasionally ask the student to have parents call the teachers rather than always having the teachers contact the parents.

- Set up an idea exchange in the school newsletter. Ask parents and/or staff to send in ideas.

- Involve parents/families in discussions about middle school while their children are still in elementary school. Do the same for the transition from middle to high school.

- Meet with schools near you and exchange ideas among the Parent Teams and/or the SPMTs.

- Conduct surveys and provide families with research topics related to raising children in today's world.

Event Planning Strategies

- Vary the times for Open Houses—hold some in the afternoon, some in the morning, and some at night.

- Hold a "Senior Citizen's Day" at the school, inviting grandparents and other older friends to the school. Provide transportation.

- Invite new staff and new families to take a tour of the district. Cover points of interest, local churches, facilities available in the area, places that could be used for field trips, boundaries of the attendance area.

- Arrange athletic and academic contests for parents to get together with other parents. Allow time afterwards for discussions about school programs.

- Have children prepare a luncheon for families, teachers, and themselves. Send handwritten invitations.

- Start "Saturday Clubs" at the school to provide enrichment programs, film showings, family recreational activities.

- During events involving food, such as a spaghetti dinner/ice cream social/international dinner/day, the key question is: While having everyone present, how will the staff interact with the families to deepen the relationships? How will the event be connected to the teaching and learning components?

- Other ideas for events include the following: male significant other/student or female significant other/student breakfast or luncheon, staff/parent dances, family movie night, health fair, curriculum showcase, dinner theater, book fair or book discussion clubs, holiday party, monthly grade-level programs, career day, carnival, yard sale or flea market with community, school beautification day, family showcase highlighting families, parent/guardian recognition day.

- Survey the needs of families. Consider setting up ESOL classes, GED classes, or community college extension courses at the school.

Engaging Volunteers

- Use parents/family members as field trip helpers and observers.
- Establish a classroom speaker's bureau with parents or relatives of students sharing their experiences, hobbies, job information. You do not have to wait until Career Day.
- Recruit parents to spend an hour or two during the year to help in their child's classroom or help in some way at home. Try not to overwhelm parents by expecting them to do everything.
- Use volunteers to serve as tutors.
- Ask families to help in the media center.
- Ask families to serve on all committees.

(Continued)

Figure 10.11 (Continued)

Classroom Strategies

- Set goals for each child with the child and parent together.

- Set up parent conferences at a variety of times to meet the needs of the families you serve.

- Have students interview their family members or parents about how life has changed since their childhood.

- Involve students in the SDP process. Have them survey their families to collect ideas for improvement (working through the Parent Team and SPMT).

- Assign homework that is relevant to the child's concrete world and will provide the practice a child needs to internalize new knowledge.

- At Back to School Night, bring a suitcase or trunk with items that demonstrate who you are and what matters to you. As a way of introduction, unpack your trunk and share who you are, using your pictures, mementos, etc. Ask each family to introduce themselves to the others. Build a team on that first night. (The same could be done with your students.)

- At the beginning of the year, take a picture of each student. By Back to School Night, display them with a large sign welcoming the families and guardians. Before that night, have the students write a note home inviting their parents to attend. This is a good idea in general—involving the students in encouraging their parents/families to participate in a variety of events by writing notes and also thank yous. Have students leave a special note in their desks for their parents the night of Back to School Night.

- Put the names of all your students in a jar. Once a week, pull a name out and call that student's family, giving them a positive progress review. While you are speaking to the parents, share other information about upcoming events at school, etc. Nothing beats a personal invitation.

- Some schools have a Family of the Month from every grade level. Children's names are drawn at random from every grade level each month. The children take home a Polaroid camera and take several pictures of their family and fill out a form that speaks to what the family enjoys and values.

- Have students lead the open houses. Have the students stand before their parents on Back to School Night or open houses and explain what they are learning and why. They can also be the greeters.

- Have students collect coupons from newspapers of at least 10 items needed at home. Ask the students to (1) go to the store with their families, (2) find the items on the coupon, (3) compute the cost with and without the coupon, and (4) compute the total savings.

- During Fire Safety Week, ask students to draw the floor plans of their homes, locating all safe exits, and to speak with their families about this.

- Invite parents and families in to learn ways they can work with math, science, language arts, and science while eating out, taking trips, watching TV together, cleaning up, etc.

Figure 10.12 Key points to consider in organizing and maintaining an effective and dynamic home-school partnership

---

An Effective and Dynamic Home-School Partnership . . .

- Includes all six types of involvement:

  Parenting

  Communicating

  Volunteering

  Learning at home

  Decision making and advocacy

  Collaborating with the community

- Reflects three levels of participation:

  Level I: Broad participation and general support

  Level II: Active daily participation in the schools

  Level III: Participation in school management

- Is guided by a shared vision built upon policy.

- Is well planned, comprehensive, and long lasting.

- Is more than a series of events.

- Provides activities that build upon each other to foster increasing degrees of involvement over time; activities are not one-time events.

- Provides opportunities for all parents/families regardless of their literacy level or native language.

- Is tailored to the specific school site population.

- Fosters relationships between parents, children, and staff. Changes in the nature and amount of parent-child interaction have been linked to changes in child behavior and achievement.

- Offers families strategies for connecting what happens at school to what happens at home in order to convey value for learning and support for student achievement.

- Encourages partnerships among schools, families, and communities.

- Enhances a successful program. DOES NOT substitute for good teaching.

SOURCE: Courtesy of Bea Fernandez, Melissa Whipple, and Jeana Preston, Parent Involvement Department, San Diego City Schools.

To sum up, in Figure 10.12 we draw your attention to a list of factors (Parent Involvement Department, San Diego City Schools, 1997) essential to organizing and maintaining an effective and dynamic home-school partnership. Let these "key points" guide the work you do.

REFERENCES

Parent Involvement Center. (1990). *Ten truths of parent involvement: A workshop for use in Chapter 1 technical assistance.* Hampton, NH: RMC Research Corporation.

Parent Involvement Department of the San Diego City Schools. (1997). *Teamwork makes the dream work: Families and schools together,* Unpublished, Part 2, p. 8.

Perrin, K. (1985). *National leadership camp: Leadership curriculum guide.* Reston, VA: National Association of Secondary School Principals, Division of Student Activities, pp. 8–10.

READ MORE ABOUT . . .

For a full discussion on children and schools, see "The School Is Preventive and Promotive," Chapter 1 in *Six Pathways to Healthy Child Development and Academic Success: The Field Guide to Comer Schools in Action* in this series.

For a bibliography of team-building exercises and ice breakers, see "Teaming and Team Building," Chapter 9 in *Six Pathways to Healthy Child Development and Academic Success* in this series.

AUTHORS' NOTE: The authors gratefully acknowledge the editorial assistance of Beverly Crowther in the preparation of this chapter.

11

The Student and Staff Support Team and the Coordination of Student Services

"Nine Different People Were Helping One Child"

William T. Brown and Sherrie Berrien Joseph

The Student and Staff Support Team (SSST) is essential to solving individual and whole-school issues that can undermine student learning and development. This chapter discusses the composition of the SSST, strategies for dealing with individual and schoolwide problems, organization, and inter-team relationships. Detailed forms developed by an extremely effective SSST in Brooklyn, New York, provide additional models for productive action.

In many ways, what we now know as the School Development Program began with the Mental Health Team, the progenitor of the Student and Staff Support Team (SSST). The late Dr. Albert Solnit, the former director of the Yale Child

Study Center, and Mr. Samuel Nash, director of special projects for the New Haven Public Schools, had recognized that clinicians and educators had much to offer each other:

> In 1966, after more than 15 years of providing periodic consultation and in-service training in public schools, as clinical and educational scholars we planned to establish a systematic long-term collaborative exchange between a clinical center and two primary schools. . . . The clinicians knew that being able to observe children in the public schools would expose them to learning about a large sector of child life that otherwise they usually heard about only in an indirect fashion. The educators knew that clinicians used certain . . . constructs and observational methods to understand the ailing child, which, when translated into an understanding of healthy or normal children, could be useful to teachers in their work with children and their parents. (Nash & Solnit, 1993, pp. xv–xvi)

Dr. Solnit then recruited a very bright and promising child psychiatrist, Dr. James P. Comer, to develop this new collaborative between the Child Study Center and the New Haven Public Schools and to be the director of its first Mental Health Team.

Over the years, school systems have generally developed the capacity to provide assessment and therapeutic services for themselves, but despite the presence of thousands of mental health professionals in the schools, there still often exists a rift between the mission of clinicians and the missions of the educators. In large part, this rift can be attributed to differential emphasis by educators and clinicians on different aspects of development: Educators are often more focused on the cognitive and linguistic development of their students; clinicians, depending on their professional training, pay relatively more attention to the physical, psychological, and social functioning of their clients.

In the Comer Process, it is the role of the SSST to actively unite the whole school community in order to promote the development of children and adolescents along *all* the developmental pathways. The SSST is charged with, first of all, the task of enabling students (as well as their teachers and families) to overcome the barriers to their learning by mobilizing the resources of the school, the district, and the surrounding community to meet the developmental needs of the students. To fulfill this role the team must possess a level of expertise in child development theory and practice that is not usually characteristic of other groups within the school community. The SSST is also charged with helping the adults in the school community change how they view students and families and how they serve them.

SSST COMPOSITION

The membership of the SSST includes those individuals in the school community who possess specialized knowledge, training, or expertise in mental health or child and adolescent development theory and practice. It is important that the members of the SSST have (or have access to) expertise in how children and youth develop along all the pathways: physical, cognitive, psychological, language, social, and ethical. More specifically, the team should include some combination of the following individuals:

- *Administrator.* The principal (or an assistant or vice-principal) is a required member of the SSST. This person is able to inform the team of the administrative and legal constraints and opportunities that may impact any interventions or programming the SSST decides to recommend.

- *Psychologist.* Most of the time, the school psychologist is responsible for the assessments conducted for special education. More generally, however, psychologists are trained in observing and understanding human behavior and, depending on their training, can contribute expertise in psychological and social development, as well as in therapeutic interventions.

- *Social workers and counselors.* In addition to their training in therapeutic techniques, social workers and counselors are often trained in accessing service systems and community resources. The ecological perspective a social worker can bring is important for identifying and intervening with both individual and global issues.

- *Special education teachers.* These teachers have specialized training in helping students to overcome barriers—including physical, emotional, and social ones—to their learning. Among the major contributions that special education teachers often make to the work of the SSST are the intervention and problem-solving skills that can benefit almost any student, regardless of education placement.

- *School nurse.* Nurses and other medically trained personnel can provide to the SSST specialized knowledge in young people's physical functioning and development, which impacts all the other areas of development.

- *Speech/hearing specialists and bilingual teachers.* These individuals provide the expertise in language development and, perhaps, physical development. Similar to the special education teacher, these team members can contribute strategies and interventions that may even help students who do not suffer from a speech, hearing, or other language impairment.

This list is by no means exclusive, and almost any individual with developmental expertise (e.g., a physical education teacher with knowledge of children's physical development) is eligible to sit on the SSST. Schools have also included community members (e.g., a member of the local community policing program) on their SSST. It is important to note that while parents or guardians are not regular members of the SSST (this is the only team in the Comer Process that does not include them as standing members), the parent or guardian of any student referred to the SSST should be included whenever possible in discussions of that student. Regular education teachers may also sit on the SSST, and the teachers who refer any student should attend, like the parent or guardian, any meetings during which the team will discuss that particular student's case.

The activities of the SSST fall into three major categories: interventions and case management for individual students, prevention and addressing global issues, and staff development.

INTERVENTIONS AND CASE MANAGEMENT FOR INDIVIDUAL STUDENTS

One of the most significant and visible SSST activities is developing interventions for individual students who are experiencing problems in their school functioning.

Although some schools use the SSST as the level of intervention prior to a special education referral, it is important to note that referral to the SSST is not just for special education students. Any student who is experiencing a barrier to or problem with their development or learning is eligible for referral to the SSST.

At times, these barriers or problems may be centered "within" the child. For example, the child may be too shy or anxious to participate in classroom activities, and the best efforts of the classroom teacher have not been enough to engage the child satisfactorily. The barrier may also be some condition outside the child's influence or control. Parents who are experiencing a great deal of financial hardship and whose work schedules are irregular, or who may be overwhelmed by having to care for several children or a gravely ill relative, may not be able to consistently prepare their children for school. More often, the problem is a result of a combination of child characteristics and contextual factors, and it is important not only that the SSST view the child through the developmental lens, but that they also adopt an ecological view of the child's behavior in that child's context.

For example, when I (W. Brown) served as a counselor in elementary schools that served a diverse but impoverished student population, I often had to work with children who were labeled as "aggressive" because they often fought with their peers. When I talked with them about their behavior, a common response was, "My mother told me that if someone hits me, I hit them back." These kids, in fact, came from rough neighborhoods where perceived weakness could lead to continued provocation and harassment or could even prove fatal when they got older. To contradict the child's parent would serve no good purpose, and my response instead was to ask two questions: "When you go to McDonald's, do you go in the back and fix your own food?" and "When you are at home, do you pay your mother for the things you eat?" Even kindergartners could understand that different settings called for different behaviors and that the expectations at school were different from those at home or in the neighborhood. Without an ecological view, this intervention would not even have occurred to me.

Referrals

There should be a very clear and structured process for referring students to the SSST. At a minimum, the referring teacher should be asked to provide a non-judgmental description of the student's challenges and strengths along the six developmental pathways. This description should also include the frequency, severity, and duration of the challenging behavior, as well as possible antecedents. Referring teachers should also indicate what intervention strategies they have already tried and the extent to which these have been effective—even if only marginally. Whenever possible, the referring teacher should also provide whatever background information (e.g., parental report of imminent divorce) or current indicators (e.g., work samples, distressing pictures or drawings) might be relevant.

Once a child has been referred to the SSST, he or she should be placed on the agenda as quickly as possible. Parents or guardians should be informed of the referral and invited to attend the meeting during which their child is being discussed. In many instances, parents are willing to take the time to come to the school, but in cases where the parents have not been able to attend, SSSTs at various Comer schools have found creative ways to include them, including making conference calls or holding the meeting at times more convenient for the parent.

Viewing the Child Through a Developmental Lens

During discussion of the child, the SSST should use a "developmental lens" and identify areas of appropriate development, overdevelopment, or underdevelopment. Specifically, the team should describe and discuss each area of the child's development and how that child's level of development might contribute to the presenting problem. *The importance of these developmental discussions cannot be stressed enough.* They are the fundamental, central process of the SSST's operation, and talking about the child in this way will yield at least two important benefits: First, the team will be more likely to gather important information that would inform possible interventions, or at least identify gaps in the team's knowledge of the child. Second, the team will be less likely to judge or label the child, and thus less likely to apply inappropriate interventions as a result of emotionally charged perceptions.

Developmentally Appropriate Interventions

Likewise, the SSST should attempt to generate interventions that are developmentally appropriate and informed. There are at least three possible levels of intervention: by the teacher within the classroom, through consultation with other school personnel, and through outside services.

The First Level of Intervention Is the Classroom

Members of the SSST should assist the referring teacher in creating and implementing strategies the teacher has not tried or thought of, or should assist the referring teacher in refining interventions already being employed.

The Second Level of Intervention Is Mobilizing School Resources

At this level, other school personnel may be called in to consult with the SSST and referring teacher. These personnel may be members of the SSST or they may be other members of the school community. In several cases we have observed, the consultant is a very experienced teacher who lends the benefit of her knowledge to the team. In other cases, a teacher who is familiar with the child and/or the child's family from another time or setting (e.g., has had a sibling in another class) provides the consultation.

The Third Level of Intervention Is Accessing Resources or Services From Outside the School

The SSST may determine that the referred child and/or the child's family might benefit from psychotherapy, substance abuse treatment, a full medical evaluation, structured activity outside of the school, or any of a number of services that the school cannot provide. In this case, the responsibility of the SSST is to coordinate these services with those the school provides and to supervise the delivery of any services provided within the school by these outside agencies or organizations. This coordination may be as important as the presence of the services themselves. In person, print, and presentations, Dr. Comer has often described a situation he encountered during the initial Baldwin-King Project in which nine different people—including social workers, psychologists, and special education teachers—were helping a single child but were not communicating with each other (Comer, Haynes, & Joyner, 1996). As a result of this lack of communication, there was neither a coherent picture of the child's needs nor a cohesive effort toward meeting those needs.

The Case Manager

After the team has discussed the case and interventions, the SSST should assign a case manager to the student. The case manager is responsible for monitoring the implementation of the recommended interventions and the progress of the referred student. It is important to note that the case manager is not necessarily responsible for conducting the intervention. For example, if the SSST recommends that psychological assessment be conducted, the psychologist does not necessarily serve as the case manager (in fact, collaboration is increased if the case manager is not the person most closely associated with the intervention). Finally, the team should review and evaluate each case periodically (we recommend reviewing cases within a month's time) and have procedures in place for closing cases that either have been resolved or need to be referred for interventions beyond the scope of the team (e.g., psychiatric hospitalization).

PREVENTION AND GLOBAL ISSUES

Just as important as meeting individual student needs (generally a form of tertiary prevention) is the SSST's role in spearheading the major preventive efforts of the school and addressing global concerns that affect the entire school community. In medicine and mental health, there are three types of prevention—primary, secondary, and tertiary—and the SSST should consider all of them.

Primary, Secondary, and Tertiary Prevention

• *Primary prevention* entails solving problems before they even occur. Vaccinations, for example, are provided to everyone and eliminate the potential problem of a specific disease.

• *Secondary prevention* is aimed at preventing problems from manifesting themselves after risks have been identified. Secondary prevention interventions are directed toward all members of a risk group. For example, children who have been retained in school are at higher risk for dropping out of school later, so a school might direct a drop-out prevention program toward anyone who is retained in their current grade for the next school year.

• *Tertiary prevention* (also known as rehabilitation) occurs after a problem has manifested itself. With tertiary prevention, the goal is to treat the problem and restore functioning. While tertiary prevention is typically more visible and demonstrable than primary or secondary prevention (and thus often more satisfying for the clinician and easier to justify with respect to costs and effort), it also tends to be the most expensive form of prevention in the long run—hence the saying, "An ounce of prevention is worth a pound of cure." Schools, just like many of our society's other institutions, are unfortunately often reactive instead of proactive with respect to many problems. They are so busy handling the day-to-day tasks of educating millions of children nationwide that they do not devote enough time, effort, and resources to primary preventive efforts.

Addressing Global Issues

We advocate that schools in general, and the SSST in particular, should consider adopting primary prevention strategies whenever possible, so that individual incidents do not develop into schoolwide issues and so that school community issues do not develop into major crises. The SSST may look in a number of directions to identify these global issues (see Figure 11.1).

Figure 11.1   Examples of possible global issues

Tardiness	Student-staff relationships
Absenteeism	Staff-parent relationships
Behavior/discipline	Response to crises or trauma
New students/school adjustment	Teacher burn-out
Learning styles	Low staff morale
Student achievement	Child neglect & abuse
Diversity/multicultural issues	Student and staff health awareness
Student interpersonal relationships	

- One source is from the individual cases that are referred to the SSST. It is often found that several cases may have commonalties or similar patterns that suggest that an intervention broader than working with individual students is warranted. For example, the SSST may find that many of the students are referred for fighting and that many of these fights start with name-calling and teasing. The team may then decide to recommend a program that emphasizes respect for peers.

- A second possible source of global issues are events, both expected and unexpected, which impact the entire school community. The response of schools to young people's needs for comfort and reassurance after the terrorist attacks on New York and Washington is a perfect example of an unexpected event. Other examples include natural disasters or the departure or death of a teacher or school administrator. Unexpected events need not be negative or tragic—the SSST may capitalize on resources suddenly becoming available for the school or advocate broadening the recognition of some scholastic or athletic achievement by the students so that the positive impact is felt throughout the school. Expected or predictable events include many of the transitions associated with the schooling process (e.g., attending a new school).

- A third source of global issues is the normal development of the students in the school. For example, although children are perfectly capable of discerning differences between people's physical features, they typically do not begin to exhibit systematic differential attitudes toward people of different races or ethnicities until six or seven years of age. This is also when students enter school and begin to observe how a societal institution—the school—treats different groups of people. Given this knowledge, the SSST may facilitate the school community, paying particular attention to issues of diversity and equitable treatment.

Similarly, students who are entering adolescence (typically around seventh grade) are beginning to grapple with issues of adolescent identity, and a major part of this process is adopting and experimenting with different roles in relationships with adults and each other. From a developmental point of view, students' defiance of adult authority might also be conceptualized as experimenting with their own exercise of power. Not coincidentally, it is at about this age that friendship groups based on convenience begin to give way to crowds and cliques based on the students' own perceptions and preferences; it is also at about this age that these groups begin more systematically to exercise social power. The SSST might then look for ways to involve the students in exercising authority within the school in appropriate and prosocial ways.

STAFF DEVELOPMENT

As effective as the SSST may be in promoting development and in prevention or intervention with individual students, the school will not be best served if developmental knowledge and expertise is concentrated within this team. The SSST is expected to help enhance the school's ability to think developmentally and use this knowledge to improve the school's climate and young people's outcomes.

For example, the clinical presentation of several psychiatric disorders in young people often differs from that of adults. In the case of depression—a very common diagnosis among both young people and adults—children and adolescents may not exhibit the depressed mood that is commonly associated with adult depression. They may, in fact, present with a very irritable mood. Knowledge of these developmental differences may influence how a teacher or administrator chooses to act toward a student who "always has an attitude" or is otherwise acting out in the school.

Members of the SSST may choose to share their clinical and developmental expertise directly with colleagues during staff development sessions. In fact, we encourage collaborative presentations that integrate the clinical perspective of the clinicians on the SSST and the education perspective of the teachers on the team or the staff. If necessary, the SSST can arrange to bring in an outside consultant or expert to provide staff development. The SSST should make clear to the staff how each staff development effort is tied into the larger mission of the team and the school, as well as the global issues the SSST has identified.

KEY POINTS ON MEETING ORGANIZATION AND PROCESS

Given the nature of the work of the SSST, there are several important points that the team must consider (see Figure 11.2): consistency, collaboration, early intervention, and confidentiality.

Figure 11.2 Some general guidelines for SSST meetings

Be Stable and Consistent

- Meet weekly for 1½ to 2 hours. Some teams meet biweekly for a longer period of time in order to accommodate the schedules and caseloads of their members.

- Establish and/or re-establish your membership early in the school year. The principal should work with the school district's Specialized Student Support Services or Special Education Department to identify support services staff who can commit to the team.

Be Organized and Thorough

- Establish an agenda for every meeting. At minimum the agenda should include a team builder, new cases, updates or status reports on previous cases, global issues, SPMT report, professional development, and sharing/development of resources.

- Establish roles for the team. We recommend that the chairperson serve for at least a school year. The other roles can rotate on a pre-established timeline.

- Establish operating procedures for the team: when, where, and how often the team meets. This information should be stabilized as soon as possible. We realize that some teams may need to experiment with meeting times, days, and locations initially; but this should become stable within 1 to 2 months.

Encourage Early Referrals and Identify
Global Issues Through Well-Known, Clear Processes

- Establish a referral process and flow chart and yearly present them to the whole school community so that everyone will know the process for bringing a student to the attention of the SSST.

- Develop or adapt referral forms, form letters, and/or other documents needed by the team. Establish a location for these forms that is known to all team members.

- Encourage members of the school community to make referrals earlier in the year, rather than later.

- Identify professional development needed by the SSST and arrange to have it provided during the meeting or at other times set aside for professional development.

- Develop written procedures for how the SSST will identify global issues. Global issues impact groups of students and/or the school as a whole, or they emerge from a study of patterns observed in the types of referrals received by the team.

Respect Confidentiality

- Find a meeting location that affords the team as much privacy as possible because of the confidential nature of the information discussed.

- Develop consent forms for parents and guardians to review and sign.

- Make sure confidential information is not overheard or included in school records that might be seen by others.

Consistency

First, consistency is absolutely essential in order for the SSST to be effective. It is important that the team meet regularly. We recommend that it meet at least weekly for 1 ½ to 2 hours. Some schools' SSSTs meet more often for a shorter period of time, or less often or for a longer period of time, depending on their caseload and the schedules of their members. Given the level of coordination and follow-up that the team's activities require, consistent attendance is vital, and the dates and times chosen for the meetings should be acceptable to all members of the team. The membership of the SSST should also be relatively stable. This is an important point to emphasize for the school administrators. The SSST is best served when the same administrator serves on the team, although it is perfectly acceptable to send a substitute if that person cannot attend.

Collaborative Problem Solving

Second, like all of the other team meetings, there should be a written agenda for each SSST meeting and adherence to consensus, collaboration, and no-fault, and effective group roles (e.g., chairperson, facilitator, notetaker, timekeeper, etc.) should be adopted to make maximum use of the time available.

Early Intervention

Third, we encourage members of the school community to make referrals earlier in the year, rather than later (members of the Special Education community understand this practice well). This practice is consistent with the idea of early intervention as a possible way to prevent later problems. Furthermore, interventions with students are likely to take some time to work, and if students are referred to the SSST later in the year, there may not be time to implement the interventions suggested by the team, evaluate their effectiveness, or refine them if they do not work. Even more important, neither the student, the teacher, nor the class is well served if the student is allowed to languish in a situation that can very well be corrected.

Confidentiality

The fourth major consideration for the SSST is that of confidentiality. Clinicians have clear ethical obligations to protect the confidentiality of their clients, and the responsibilities associated with these obligations are part of their professional education and training. Although school records are also confidential, clinical records are generally afforded greater protection. As a consequence, it is important that every member of the SSST understand both the importance of confidentiality and the specific measures the group will adopt to protect it.

The team should develop consent forms for parents and guardians to review and sign. The team should meet on school premises so that they have access to any necessary school records and so that confidential information will not be overheard in a public setting. Some of the information that the SSST gathers *must not* be included in the school record, and the SPMT and the larger school community must understand that members of the SSST *cannot* share all the information at their disposal.

RELATIONSHIP WITH THE OTHER TEAMS

As depicted in the "Schoolhouse" diagram (Figure 2.2 in Chapter 2), there should be consistent communication among the SSST, the SPMT, and the Parent Team. If the SPMT is the engine of the school, then the SSST is the sensor array and dashboard panel: It monitors the functioning of the school and provides feedback when things are going wrong.

Generally speaking, the SSST is responsible for informing the SPMT of global issues it has identified and for making recommendations to address them. Once the SPMT has decided on a course of action, the SSST then acts to implement the SPMT's policy decision. Ideally, the SSST does not work in isolation, but instead works with one or more of the SPMT's subcommittees (e.g., Climate, Curriculum, Instruction and Assessment, Public Relations) to implement the prevention or programmatic effort. At least one member of the SSST sits on the SPMT to represent the team and its perspectives and to carry information from the SPMT to the SSST. Given the diversity of concerns that face the SPMT, the SSST representative should function as the "voice for development" in the meetings, just as the entire team should act as the voice for development for the entire school.

The relationship of the SSST and the Parent Team likewise involves a great deal of communication between the groups, but that communication may be more diverse and informal. Often, the SSST will serve as the first contact a student's family will have with the school. Members of the SSST may be experts on child development, but parents and guardians are the experts on *their* child's development. The SSST represents the school, and so must make conscious and sustained efforts to attempt to form collaborative partnerships with parents and community members. The SSST may also lend support to Parent Team activities or provide training and consultation to the Parent Team.

While the information presented above represents the ideal of SSST functioning, schools have developed their SSSTs in different ways, depending on a variety of factors, including their needs and the resources available to them.

MODEL FORMS

The Model Forms section of this chapter provides a variety of ready-to-use forms that can be used for productive action.

The forms in Figures 11.3–11.12 were created by the SSST at Public School 46, the Edward C. Blum Elementary School, in Community School District 13, Brooklyn, New York. They appear here courtesy of Principal Carmen S. Gonzalez and the school's SSST.

REFERENCES

Comer, J. P., Haynes, N. M., & Joyner, E. (1996). The School Development Program. In J. P. Comer, N. M. Haynes, & E. T. Joyner (Eds.), *Rallying the whole village: The Comer Process for reforming education* (pp. 1–26). New York: Teachers College Press.

Nash, S., & Solnit, A. J. (1993). Introduction. In J. P. Comer (Ed.), *School power: Implications of an intervention project* (2nd ed., pp. xiii–xix). New York: Free Press.

Figure 11.3   Child study team—Student form

Child Study Team — Student Form

Edward C. Blum Elementary School – Public School 46
Carmen S. Gonzalez, Principal

Name _____

Date _____

Time of Incident _____

This is the classroom rule I did not follow:

_____

_____

This is what happened:

_____

_____

_____

This is why I did it:

_____

_____

_____

This is what I could have done:

_____

_____

_____

Teacher's Comments (relate to developmental pathways framework):

_____

_____

_____

Other Comments:

_____

_____

_____

Student Signature _____   Date _____

Teacher Signature _____   Date _____

SOURCE: Courtesy of Public School 46, the Edward C. Blum Elementary School, Carmen S. Gonzalez, Principal.

Figure 11.4 Child study team

Child Study Team

Edward C. Blum Elementary School – Public School 46
Carmen S. Gonzalez, Principal

MEETING FLOW		DATE _____
Case Overview (Pathway category focus)		
Follow up Case Reviews Medical/status pending (5 minutes)	New Case Reviews Pathway/Action plan (15 minutes per case)	Discussion of scheduled activities/workshops (5 minutes)
Global Issues		
Conclusions (Comer moment/team process/observations/praises/recommendations)		

SOURCE: Courtesy of Public School 46, the Edward C. Blum Elementary School, Carmen S. Gonzalez, Principal.

Figure 11.5   Child study referral notice

Child Study Referral Notice

Edward C. Blum Elementary School
Public School 46 – CSD 13
100 Clermont Avenue, Brooklyn NY 11205
(718) 834-7694 Fax # (718) 243-0726

School Personnel: Please use this form to inform the parent of his/her child's referral to the Child Study Team

STUDENT'S NAME	DATE
TEACHER	GRADE/CLASS

PARENT/GUARDIAN REFERRAL NOTIFICATION

We are sure that you share our concern that your child's school performance is not as positive as we might expect. To better understand any reasons behind this situation, your child has been referred to the Child Study Team. The process of this referral and the purpose of this referral are:

➢ Review current and past records and investigate patterns, changes in performance or other factors that attribute to present performance levels.

➢ Conduct student, parent and teacher interviews to gain background information.

➢ Bring together key personnel that would assist with the discussion of interventions to improve your child's performance.

➢ Monitor and assess the value of any intervention strategies already in place.

➢ Determine the need for in-depth student evaluation to better understand and address concerns.

*We hope that you will be able to be as involved as possible in this very important process. We have scheduled an appointment for you to meet with the Child Study Team on:

(*Day of Week*) _____   (*Month*) _____   (*Date*) _____   (*Year*) _____   at (*Time*) _____

Presently, the school has concerns about your child's performance in the area(s) checked below:

❑ Academic Progress   ❑ Skill Retention   ❑ Socialization   ❑ Attention
❑ Behavior   ❑ Aggression   ❑ Speech/Language   ❑ Homework
❑ Hearing/Vision   ❑ Attendance   ❑ Health _____   ❑ Other _____

Additional Comments

PARENT/GUARDIAN ACKNOWLEDGMENT SECTION

It is our intent to keep you informed and involved in your child's performance at school. Please return this parent acknowledgement section to the Child Study Team or your child's teacher so that we may begin serving your child's needs.

TO CHILD STUDY TEAM OF PS 46

❑ I have received and read the Parent/Guardian Referral Notification. I understand that the school is very concerned about my child's performance at school and is seeking strategies to assist my child.

❑ I am aware of this situation and will meet with the Child Study Team on the scheduled appointment.
❑ I am aware of this situation, however, I am unable to attend on the scheduled date. I am able to attend the Child Study Team conference on

(date) _____ at (time) _____

Parent/Guardian signature (required) _____   Date _____

SOURCE: Courtesy of Public School 46, the Edward C. Blum Elementary School, Carmen S. Gonzalez, Principal.

Figure 11.6 Referral

Referral

Edward C. Blum Elementary School
Public School 46 – CSD 13
100 Clermont Avenue, Brooklyn NY 11205
(718) 834-7694 Fax # (718) 243-0726

School Personnel: Please use this form to initiate the process of referring a student for Academic or Social Intervention Services.
 This is an important initial step in the consideration of child's eligibility for additional services and a possible IEP.

STUDENT INFORMATION			**REFERRING PERSONNEL**

_____   _____   _____   _____

STUDENT'S NAME   DATE   CLASS   REFERRING TEACHER/ADMINISTOR

Presently the student's performance is:

❑ Passing   ❑ At Risk   ❑ Failing

_____   _____

Signature   Date

At this time, concerns about this student are: Has the parent been made aware of your concern? ❑ Yes   ❑ No

❑ Recently Identified   ❑ Ongoing and Serious   How ❑ Parent Conference   ❑ Phone Call   ❑ Letter(s)

Area(s) of Concern: ❑ Other

❑ Academic Progress	❑ Skill Retention	Have you ever attached the required supporting documentation
❑ Socialization	❑ Behavior	for case review? ❑ Yes ❑ No
❑ Attention	❑ Aggression	
❑ Speech/Language	❑ Homework	List documentation attached to this request
❑ Hearing/Vision	❑ Attendance	_____
❑ Health	❑ Other	_____

Services student is already receiving: Identify Actions/Interventions already initiated:

❑ Reading	❑ Math	❑ Speech	❑ Parent Conference	❑ Student Conference
❑ ESL/BL	❑ Counseling	❑ Medical	❑ Record Review	❑ Special Seating
❑ Social Work	❑ Peer Mediation		❑ Modified Instruction	❑ Buddy/Peer
❑ Psychological	❑ Other		❑ Behavior Plan	❑ Skill Inventory
			❑ Daily Progress Form	❑ Counseling
			❑ Other	

COMMENTS:

_____

_____

_____

_____

_____

White page – Child Study Team   Canary page – Teacher Copy   Pink page – Administration Copy

SOURCE: Courtesy of Public School 46, the Edward C. Blum Elementary School, Carmen S. Gonzalez, Principal.

Figure 11.7 Child study action sheet, Side 1

Child Study Action Sheet — Side 1

Edward C. Blum Elementary School
Public School 46 – CSD 13
100 Clermont Avenue, Brooklyn NY 11205
(718) 834-7694 Fax # (718) 243-0726

SUDENT'S NAME _____ CLASS _____

Teacher _____ Case Manager _____

Conference Date _____ Case Review Date _____

PATHWAY	INDICATORS	RECOMMENDED ACTION	START DATE/ END DATE
PHYSICAL	• Physical health • Nutrition • Exercise • Responsible decision making	[ ] Medical exam [ ] Vision/hearing screening [ ] Nutrition conference [ ] Open Airways class [ ] Other	
COGNITIVE	• Flexibility of thought • Logical thinking • Manipulate information • Interaction with environment • Basic academic skills • Ability to adapt to environment	[ ] Class observation [ ] Teacher conference [ ] Home visit [ ] AIS Services [ ] Staff development [ ] Informal evaluation [ ] New class placement [ ] Peer tutor [ ] Other	
PSYCHOLOGICAL	• Feelings of adequacy • Managing emotions • Accepting differences • Self-esteem	[ ] Class observation [ ] Home visit [ ] Agency referral [ ] Psychological evaluation [ ] Counseling	
LANGUAGE	• Receptive language • Expressive language • Process communication	[ ] Informational evaluation [ ] Formal evaluation [ ] Class observation	
SOCIAL	• Empathy • Communication skills • Good relationships • Group interactions	[ ] Class observation [ ] Teacher conference [ ] New class placement [ ] In-house intervention [ ] School service [ ] Counseling [ ] Peer mediation [ ] Daily Progress report [ ] Staff development	
ETHICAL	• Appropriate behaviors • Respect self • Respect others • Sound decision-making	[ ] Class observation [ ] Peer mediation [ ] Counseling [ ] School service [ ] Agency referral	

SOURCE: Courtesy of Public School 46, the Edward C. Blum Elementary School, Carmen S. Gonzalez, Principal.

Figure 11.8   Child study action sheet, Side 2

Child Study Action Sheet — Side 2

Issue		
Pathway	Assessment	Intervention
Physical		
Cognitive		
Psychological		
Language		
Social		
Ethical		

SOURCE: Courtesy of Public School 46, the Edward C. Blum Elementary School, Carmen S. Gonzalez, Principal.

Figure 11.9 Child Study Team—Strategies to improve the school

Child Study Team

Strategies to Improve the School

Pathway	Goal	Target Group	Intervention Service(s)	Estimated #
Physical	Increase student nutritional knowledge/increase sports participation	• Overweight students • Open Airways students	• Nutrition committee • Sports Monday • Open Airways	28
Cognitive	Increase student academic activity	• Grade 3 • 6+ students	Reduced Class Size (after-school tutorial)	
Psychological	Increase student self-esteem	Identified guidance group	• Individual/Group counseling • Character Education program • Clubs	15
Language	Increase student use of appropriate language (audience)	Grades 4–6	• Monthly assembly programs • Drama club productions	48
Social	Enhance student empathy and compassion	Behavior Groups	• Counseling • Peer Mediation	50
Ethical	Enhance students' decision making for the collective good	Pre-suspended and In-house suspended students	• In-House Suspension Program • Peer Mediation • Counseling • School Service	35

SOURCE: Courtesy of Public School 46, the Edward C. Blum Elementary School, Carmen S. Gonzalez, Principal.

Figure 11.10 Child Study Team self-assessment form

Child Study Team Self-Assessment Form
Edward C. Blum Elementary School – Public School 46
Carmen S. Gonzalez, Principal

Team Leadership	Always (4)	Frequently (3)	Sometimes (2)	Never (1)
Is our vision of "all students can succeed" communicated to the parents, students, and staff?				
Do we encourage teachers to assess student learning styles and use developmentally appropriate teaching strategies?				
Do we constantly practice and apply Comer principles?				
Did we fully and fairly participate in all Child Study conferences?				
Do we make all decisions in the best interests of children?				
Resources	**Always (4)**	**Frequently (3)**	**Sometimes (2)**	**Never (1)**
Do we provide community partnerships to support students with the most needs?				
Do we seek volunteers or tutors to help all students achieve?				
Do we seek out grants or funds to support the learning needs of all our students?				
Parental Involvement	**Always (4)**	**Frequently (3)**	**Sometimes (2)**	**Never (1)**
Do we provide parents with instructional/behavioral management activities that can be used at home to reinforce positive learning?				
Do we make parents feel welcome in our school?				
Do we consider parents' work schedules and commitments when we schedule conferences?				
Do we provide parents with the appropriate standards for the child's academic/social success?				
Comprehensive Planning	**Always (4)**	**Frequently (3)**	**Sometimes (2)**	**Never (1)**
Do we involve all stakeholders in our child study plan?				
Does our plan focus on academic achievement for all students?				
Have we devoted adequate resources to fairly implement our plan for student achievement?				
Do we monitor and evaluate plan implementation to determine our degree of success?				
Do we follow up and submit all required documentation to the team case manager in a timely fashion?				

SOURCE: Courtesy of Public School 46, the Edward C. Blum Elementary School, Carmen S. Gonzalez, Principal.

Figure 11.11 Student behavioral referral (administrative)

Student Behavioral Referral (Administrative)

Edward C. Blum Elementary School
Public School 46 – CSD 13
100 Clermont Avenue, Brooklyn NY 11205
(718) 834-7694 Fax # (718) 243-0726

School personnel: Please use this form to inform the administration of a student's infraction of school rules and policy. Submit the form to the principal. Following administrative action, a copy will be returned to the teacher for the files.

STUDENT'S NAME	Grade/Class	DATE
Report Prepared By Title	Assignment/Period/Activity	

TEACHER REPORT

Description of Infraction: _____

_____

_____

_____

Previous Incidents Involving Student: _____

_____

_____

_____

Corrective Efforts: _____

_____

_____

_____

ADMINISTRATIVE ACTION TAKEN

❏ Consultation with student
❏ In-school disciplinary action
  (mandated service/exclusion from trip/exclusion from clubs, etc.)
❏ Guidance conference
❏ Superintendent's suspension

❏ After-school detention
❏ Child Study Referral
❏ Warning issued
❏ Removal from classroom
❏ Expulsion from school
❏ New classroom assigned

❏ Peer Mediation
❏ Parent conference
❏ Principal's suspension
❏ In-house suspension
❏ Review student records
❏ Office detention

COMMENTS: _____

_____

_____

Authorized Signature _____ Date _____

Student Signature _____ Date _____

SOURCE: Courtesy of Public School 46, the Edward C. Blum Elementary School, Carmen S. Gonzalez, Principal.

Figure 11.12 Parent notification—Student discipline report

Parent Notification
Student Discipline Report
Edward C. Blum Elementary School
Public School 46 – CSD 13
100 Clermont Avenue, Brooklyn NY 11205
(718) 834-7694 Fax # (718) 243-0726

School personnel: Please use this form to inform the parent of his/her child's infraction of school rules and policy. Administrative signature is required before form is sent home.		
STUDENT'S NAME	Grade/Class	Date
Report prepared by Title	Infraction/Location/Date/Time	

PARENT/GUARDIAN NOTIFICATION

This report has been prepared to notify you of your child's infraction of school policy, the corrective action taken and the recommended future action(s) that will be taken by the school. Your immediate attention and response to this report is <u>required</u>.

IDENTIFIED INFRACTION		
❏ Not wearing school uniform ❏ Not in assigned place ❏ Smoking ❏ Scholastic dishonesty ❏ Unacceptable language or gestures ❏ Violation of Internet policy ❏ Falsely activating a fire alarm ❏ Engaging in intimidation/ coercion/extortion ❏ Engaging in sexual physical aggression ❏ Committing arson	❏ Possession/selling of a controlled substance or alcohol ❏ Continuous disruptive behavior in classroom (4 or more times) ❏ Disruptive behavior ❏ Left school/class ❏ Gambling ❏ Lying ❏ Disruptive bus behavior ❏ Possession of a controlled substance	❏ Cutting class ❏ Chronic lateness ❏ Fighting ❏ Aggressive behavior ❏ Defying school authority ❏ Engaging in theft ❏ Damaging school property ❏ Possession/use of a weapon ❏ Unexcused absence
CORRECTIVE ACTION TAKEN (T)/RECOMMENDED (R)		
❏ Consultation with student ❏ In-school disciplinary action (mandated service/exclusion from clubs, etc.) ❏ Guidance conference ❏ Superintendent's suspension ❏ After-school detention	❏ Child Study referral ❏ Warning issued ❏ Removal from classroom ❏ Expulsion from school ❏ New classroom assigned ❏ Peer mediation	❏ Parent conference ❏ Principal's suspension ❏ In-house suspension ❏ Review student records ❏ Office detention

COMMENTS:

SOURCE: Courtesy of Public School 46, the Edward C. Blum Elementary School, Carmen S. Gonzalez, Principal.

12

The Student
and Staff Support
Team and Child
Development

Felicia D. Gil

The Student and Staff Support Team (SSST) works to ensure that the developmental and academic needs of every student are met. This chapter follows the journey of a Florida elementary school through implementation of the Comer Process and establishment of a Family Enrichment Center that has become a learning place for all students and their parents.

Great successes are often achieved through small steps and a slow process; such is the story of our school. The story begins in the summer of 1996, when I became principal of Charles R. Hadley Elementary School. My new school was located in a low socioeconomic area in the northwest section of Miami, Florida. The school had approximately 1250 students, in Grades pre-K–5, most of them new immigrants from many Latin American countries and the Caribbean. About 94 percent of the students were Hispanic, 45 percent of them had limited English proficiency (LEP), and about 76 percent were eligible for free or reduced-price lunch.

The school was beginning implementation of the Comer Process and was providing fragmented services to meet a wide range of students' needs. These services were being provided on a small scale and were not adequate to meet the community's needs. In a small corner of the Media Center, services were provided through the Charles Hadley Involving Parents Successfully Program. This program was a school initiative that provided instructional resources, assistance with homework, and referral to support agencies for students and parents. These services were provided by a paraprofessional for an hour every afternoon. This attempt was valuable but insufficient to meet the needs of the students and parents.

During the 1997–1998 school year, the school received Title I and Title VII funds. As a Comer school, we found these additional resources to be instrumental in providing the support to the students and staff that would facilitate each child's development in the school and provide the assistance the parents needed in order to make this a reality. Specifically, we created a Family Enrichment Center using a combination of the federal and school funds. This center has been central to our efforts to enhance the development of every child in our school.

THE WORK OF THE SSST

At the beginning of every school year, teachers are provided with an individual profile of each of our 1,250 students. This profile contains information on the English proficiency level, participation in exceptional education programs (or any other programs), reading and math levels, writing proficiency, standardized and criterion referenced test scores, and special needs of every child in the classroom.

To ensure that every child's potential is developed and individual needs are met, everyone in the school is a potential member of the Student and Staff Support Team (SSST). Who attends which SSST meeting depends on the needs being addressed. An SSST team meeting can include classroom teachers, parents, administrators, special area teachers, exceptional education teachers, a counselor, a social worker, a psychologist, and social agencies' representatives or other personnel as needed. Members of the SSST team attending specific meetings are those directly involved in the child's education and/or with vested interests in the academic program. Our team adheres to both district and state guidelines regarding confidentiality standards for student records and information.

The work of the SSST begins on the Friday prior to the opening of the school year. This is Get Acquainted Day, when the school offers an opportunity for parents to meet with school personnel. This activity allows parents to visit the school, become familiar with the school plant, and receive an orientation on school procedures before the school year begins. Another opportunity is provided on the Hadley First Day Celebration that takes place the first day of school. Students participate in a wide range of activities to establish a positive connection with the school from the outset. Parents are also invited to share in the festivities. These activities promote trust and the positive relationships that are essential among parents, students, and school personnel. During these functions an informal needs assessment is conducted, and parents share their goals and the special needs of their children.

The school provides many opportunities for the SSST to meet and share information. Students' needs are discussed at weekly grade-level meetings and monthly across-grade-level meetings. The classroom teachers and other student service personnel attend these meetings. Academic reviews are performed, and students not meeting academic and other standards are identified.

Students identified as having special needs are reviewed in-depth by the SSST. Services provided include assessments such as a language survey, academic review, and social history. Other services include tutorial classes (on Saturdays and before, during, and after school), counseling, and psychological services.

THE FAMILY ENRICHMENT CENTER

For parents to be able to help their children, we created a Family Enrichment Center to provide assistance with inservice training and on-site adult education classes. The center is staffed with a full-time teacher and four community involvement specialists. Through the center, all school services are integrated to meet the needs of the students with optimum return.

To maximize these services, the center is open daily from 7:30 a.m. to 6:00 p.m. The center provides in-service training in a wide range of topics, including benchmarks for each grading period that students at each grade level need to meet, as well as how parents can help their children with the required state tests. These workshops are provided by grade level in English and in Spanish. In addition to these services, the community involvement specialists perform periodic home visits to lend assistance to the parents, make them aware of available resources, and inform them of students' progress. We hold parent conferences regularly and schedule additional conferences every time a student is not meeting standards or is in need of special services.

MEETING THE DEVELOPMENTAL NEEDS OF STUDENTS

In order to meet the physical, social, and mental health needs of the students, the school secured the cooperation of Children's Hospital, the Children's Psychiatric Center, and Bright Horizons. The hospital provides families with free immunizations, physical check-ups, and follow-ups at school or at the hospital. The other two centers provide ongoing counseling and psychological services both at the school and at their offices to students and families who need assistance in adjusting to their new environment, coping with home and social problems, and resolving conflicts.

Academic needs are assessed and met by a team of professionals utilizing a wide range of instructional and motivational techniques, special programs, and individualized instruction. Students who do not make progress in spite of all this assistance are referred to the Child Study Team. This team is composed of the classroom teacher, the parent, the counselor, an administrator, and special area teachers and/or other professionals that the team deems necessary to best meet the child's needs. The team reviews the student's performance and needs and suggests alternative strategies to be implemented for a period of two weeks. At the end of that time, the effectiveness of the implemented strategies is assessed and recommendations are made either to continue with the suggested strategies or to employ alternative strategies, which will be revisited within three weeks.

Among the alternative strategies and services provided, we include student academic reviews with an emphasis on strengths, assessment of learning modalities, vision and hearing screenings, assessment of home environment, social and medical histories, in-school counseling for the student and the parents, assistance with homework for parents and students, parenting skills training, and referrals to mental health and medical services. If progress is not made after these strategies have been implemented and monitored for the prescribed amount of time, a complete battery of psychological testing is requested. The team then analyzes the results, and a recommendation based on the results is made for placement in the appropriate program. The SSST continues monitoring the student's progress. As soon as it is recommended, the child will be mainstreamed. Throughout this process, support and counseling are provided to the student and the family as needed.

PARENTAL PARTICIPATION

The arrival as immigrants to a new country can be stressful and a real cultural and social shock. The newcomers have to struggle with economic survival, language acquisition, and adjusting to a new way of life. At the same time as they are struggling with the new environment, they must find inner strength to support their family in surviving in this country. A feeling of isolation, helplessness, and frustration prevails among the majority of them.

Even though the school had begun the implementation of the Comer Process, parental support was fragmented and inadequate. The three guiding principles of no-fault, consensus, and collaboration needed to be extended to the parents and the community. Our work began by reaching out to one parent at a time. We established an open door policy and ensured a warm and inviting atmosphere throughout the school, and the parents began responding by becoming more involved in school affairs.

It was evident that many resources needed to be found and integrated to meet the needs of the many parents coming to school. The school has 1,250 students, and each year an average of 600 parents visit the Family Enrichment Center created as a result of this effort. The faculty wrote a grant that was funded through Title VII, and at the same time, the school received Title I funds. By integrating all these resources into the school budget, the dream of fully implementing the Comer Process became a reality.

A key factor in the success of the center was the full involvement of all stakeholders. Most important to its effectiveness was to find staff members who would buy into the Comer philosophy. A teacher who had created a parent center with me at my previous school was persuaded to embark on this venture at my new school. A critical aspect in her selection was her empathy with parents and her conviction that families are essential in developing the whole child. In turn, with the assistance of the entire staff, two parent trainers and two community involvement specialists were enlisted.

A survey was conducted among all parents not only to determine their needs but also to identify the strengths and talents they could contribute to the school. Based on the survey, in-service training was developed and services were provided. At the same time, a series of motivational techniques were implemented to maintain parent interest and involvement. The school became a learning place for all students and parents. Some motivational techniques included creating a lending library and having a monthly recognition program for students and parents who use the library. Students who read the most books are recognized on closed-circuit television, and receive a certificate and a gift from our Dade partners. Parents are rewarded for visiting the center by entering their names in a raffle for a gift donated by our Dade partners. This is also done on closed-circuit television during the monthly recognition program. Door prizes are provided for the parents who attend in-service training and meetings. To encourage parent attendance at district and regional meetings, the PTA rents a bus to provide transportation. We provide small gifts to parents and sing and play games on the bus to make trips more enjoyable. As a result, Charles R. Hadley always wins the trophy for best parent attendance at meetings.

In developing the concept of a Family Enrichment Center, we had the idea of providing an environment of peace and comfort (which sometimes is lacking in our society). We wanted the school to be a comfort zone, a safe haven for all, a home away from home, where a no-fault approach and collaboration were the keys to enter.

AN INCLUSION MODEL FOR STUDENTS WITH SPECIAL NEEDS

Being an exceptional education student can bring feelings of inadequacy and frustration to a child. Children think they are different and feel labeled. As a result, their self-concept is low and they sometimes simply give up. Struggling with this problem, and trying to provide an environment that would be supportive of children, the SSST tackled this global issue. An inclusion model was proposed. This model would provide a setting in which the special needs of these students would be met without identification or labeling. A team consisting of a regular classroom teacher and an exceptional education teacher staffed each inclusion classroom. Special care was taken to select a team whose members could complement each other and support the goals of the program. The student population of these classrooms consists of 50 percent regular students and 50 percent exceptional education students. A visitor to the classrooms would find it very difficult to distinguish the regular students from the exceptional education students. High standards are set for all students. This model has proven so successful that some students in the exceptional education inclusion classes have qualified directly for the gifted program because of their high test scores on standardized tests. A significant fact is that the regular students assigned to these classrooms are students that are unmotivated and whose academic level is below grade level. One can only imagine the quality of the instruction taking place in these classrooms and the support provided to achieve these results.

HOME LEARNING PACKAGES

Approximately 94 percent of the student population is Hispanic from many Latin American countries and the Caribbean, and their ties to their homelands tend to be very strong. Frequently, they and their families travel back to their countries for extended periods of time. In spite of this, the children are expected to achieve at the same level as students who remain in school year-round. To compound this problem, when they return, the students need a refresher course in their basic skills and in their newly acquired English language skills.

In an attempt to resolve this schoolwide concern, the SSST recommended the development of Home Learning packages that were utilized by our students to take with them to their home country. These packages have proven so successful that all students work with them during extended holidays. Students complete and return the packages upon their return to school.

CELEBRATING OUR SUCCESS

Adopting the School Development Program was instrumental in Charles R. Hadley's success story. The Comer Process provided the structure through which all school programs and services became integrated under the "Comer Umbrella." By implementing the three guiding principles and maintaining a focus on the child through the six developmental pathways, the school has received both state and national recognition.

Hadley was one of nine schools out of 372 Miami-Dade County public schools to receive a grade of A from the Florida School Accountability System during the first year that the system was implemented in 1998–1999. The school also received this grade in 2000–2001 and again in 2002–2003. For being graded A, the school obtained Florida School Recognition funds to provide incentive bonuses for employees and incentives for the students. The school was also selected to receive performance pay during the 2003–2004 school year. Three elementary schools in each of the six regional centers were selected. In our regional center there are 34 elementary schools, and Hadley was one of three selected to receive performance pay. As a result of performance pay, all instructional staff at the school will receive a stipend of 5 percent based on their salaries. In addition, the school was recognized as one of the top 20 schools in the state of Florida—one of seven in Miami-Dade County Public Schools to achieve this honor. Schools were selected for sustained academic achievement and best practices implemented at the school. Charles R. Hadley student achievement data and best practices are published on the Internet at the Web site www.floridaschoolreport.org.

These achievements are even more remarkable due to the high percentage of immigrant families and the neighborhood's low socioeconomic status. The Comer Process provided the tools by which innovation and positive interpersonal relationships have flourished, making the school a center for quality education and a place with open doors to our community, where everyone can feel welcome.

13

The Students Have Ruled: School Should Not Hurt

One Comer School's Approach to Bullying and Other Student Interpersonal Problems

William T. Brown and Rebecca Stetson Werner

The new literature on bullying reveals significant inadequacies in traditional interventions. The authors of this chapter, two clinical psychologists at the Yale Child Study Center, reflect on the School Development Program's (SDP) power to (1) break the cycle of physical and emotional violence perpetrated by bullies and those who look the other way or encourage them and (2) support effective interventions that yield only positive, intended consequences. One such intervention is a New Jersey elementary school's student-initiated and -run Student Court, described here in detail.

In the late 1990s, several incidents of school violence captured the attention of the entire nation. While violence in and around schools had been of great concern for several years (especially in urban schools and districts), the nation was unprepared for the horror of the killings that took place in Paducah, Kentucky; Jonesboro, Arkansas; Littleton, Colorado; and Encino, California. These incidents rightfully provoked a number of questions as to what would move these young people—some of them only in their early teens—to pick up firearms and murder classmates and teachers.

It did not take very long for bullying to become identified as a common thread that ran through many of these horrific events. The results from a Center for Disease Control study published in 2001 documented that bullying is a very large problem in the nation's schools. The results indicated that over half the participating students reported that they were bullied every week, and that approximately 10,000 students stayed home at least once a month because they feared bullies at their school. After the murders at Columbine in Colorado, the Secret Service conducted a study of 37 incidents of "targeted violence" in schools dating back to 1974 and concluded that in two-thirds of the cases, the perpetrators had been the victims of bullying, taunting, and/or teasing. The very simple message is that bullying hurts, and tens of thousands of young people are experiencing the pain of being physically assaulted, picked on, and ostracized by peers in our schools every single day.

As a result of these findings, many in the country began to focus on the negative impact that bullying has on their schools and communities, including the governor of Colorado, Bill Owens, who signed into state law antibullying legislation in 2000. Although it unfortunately took these high-profile killings at schools to focus the nation's attention on the problems that bullying causes, many schools and school districts responded rapidly by developing or adopting antibullying programs, and a cottage industry sprang up in response to these needs and demands. Many of these programs, however, have not integrated the most current research on bullying and aggressive behavior. Interestingly, while social scientists and psychiatrists have studied the phenomenon of aggression for decades, their work has typically focused only on physical aggression, and only recently have they begun conceptualizing and systematically studying bullying and other maladaptive ways students exert control, power, and dominance over their peers.

One of the problems with many of the antibullying programs that currently exist is that they tend—like much of the social science research—to focus on overt physical or verbal aggression and thus convey the impression that bullies are one-of-a-kind. Results from recent research are making it increasingly apparent that young people who bully can employ a range of tactics, and investigators are starting to identify different profiles of bullying and aggressive behaviors.

AGGRESSION

Two types of aggression that are receiving a great deal of research attention are physical and relational aggression. Physical aggression is behaviors that harm the victim primarily through damage or threat of damage to the victim's physical person. Relational aggression, however, refers to the behaviors that inflict harm on another young person through their peer relationships. For example, "relational bullies" may influence or convince a group of students not to be friends with another student. They may engage in this type of bullying verbally (e.g., telling their circle of friends not to like the victim) or nonverbally (e.g., rolling their eyes or turning their backs when the victim speaks, refusing to allow the victim to sit in the group).

As a result of this new appreciation for the number of ways that young people can act aggressively toward their peers, many of our assumptions regarding bullies are being challenged, especially the image of the physically larger and less socially skilled (boy) bully who intimidates and assaults smaller, weaker peers. There is evidence that some bullies, the ones who are most successful at getting other young people to do what they want, are actually very socially skilled individuals who choose to use their social sophistication to achieve their own ends rather than to be respectful of the desires and emotions of others. This "successful bully" is nonetheless still victimizing peers in a way that is both hurtful and harmful.

There is also mounting evidence that these successful bullies are conducting their bullying *in the presence of adults*. Often, they may not get caught because they are skilled enough to work when adults are occupied, inattentive, or unavailable. Worse, these students may even enjoy the tacit approval of the adults around them. While physical aggression is much easier to define, adults may not necessarily consider relationally aggressive behavior as socially inappropriate. Depending on their personal characteristics (e.g., attractiveness, scholastic achievement, school involvement), some of these bullies are well liked or even respected by their peers and adults in the schools, which makes confronting or reporting the bullying that much more difficult.

VICTIMIZATION

In addition, evidence is beginning to accumulate that young people are victimized in different ways, depending on their level of social development or other individual characteristics. For example, girls (who tend to be more socially oriented) are more likely to be victims of relational bullying, especially when they lack self-esteem or have other social adjustment problems. It appears that these girls, who tend to desire friends and companionship but have had difficulty making friends or fitting into the school's social structure, may actually be singled out by socially sophisticated bullies who exploit their vulnerabilities. The research that has been done thus far suggests that these girls actually perceive the relational bullying to be even more hurtful than physical bullying—findings analogous to those in research on adult relational abuse. Boys, however, who tend to be more activity oriented, are more likely to be victims of physical bullying, particularly when their physical development lags behind that of their peers and/or they lack the social skills necessary to navigate the school's social landscape.

Bullying is much more likely to cause adjustment problems when it is chronic and when it carries across peer groups in different settings (e.g., at school *and* in the neighborhood), as opposed to when it is an isolated event or only occurs in one aspect of the young person's life. Schools must therefore be very careful that they address bullying in a systematic and comprehensive way. In fact, if the school is successful with antibullying efforts and the rates of victimization decrease, any future acts of bullying will likely have a greater impact than when rates of bullying were high: A child who continues to be bullied after interventions have been generally helpful may feel even more isolated and singled out for victimization, and thus the negative effects of bullying will be magnified.

INTERVENTIONS

When addressing bullying in a comprehensive way, however, educators are much more at a loss when it comes to dealing with the more systemic and relational aspects of bullying. For example, the available research indicates that bringing the bully and the victim together to "work things out" is ineffective and may be even more damaging than the original bullying. Because the power differential that contributed to the bullying in the first place continues to dominate the interaction, this kind of intervention may actually support the bully's social dominance while leaving the victim in a dangerous situation. Interventions will need to appreciate the different causes and styles of bullying in order to appropriately identify and effectively intervene with both bullies and victims before the serious consequences of these behaviors occur. It is also important to recognize that those who bully are often those who have been bullied and that this disruptive, negative, and sometimes tragic behavior is an expression of poor development. Effective interventions will thus need to address not only the discrete behaviors associated with bullying, but also the other aspects of underdevelopment that contribute to the phenomenon.

From our perspective, while the students involved in the tragic and horrific incidents of school violence mentioned above might have been well developed along some of the pathways (evidenced by their abilities to plan and physically carry out their violent plans), they lacked the ethical development to refrain from inflicting so much pain on those around them. Similarly, those who tormented them also lacked enough social and ethical development to support their classmates or even to stand up for them and protect them when they were being victimized. Furthermore, we fear that there exists in many schools a climate of distrust between students and adults, in which students' making adults aware of hurtful or even dangerous behaviors is socially discouraged as "snitching" or "ratting" on one's friends or classmates.

THE ROLE OF THE SSST

In the case of bullying, the Student and Staff Support Team (SSST) has a special and critical role to play. As the team whose membership is composed primarily of individuals with expertise in child and adolescent development, the SSST is charged with the responsibility of identifying and generating possible preventive solutions to schoolwide problems. As such, the SSST should be very active in helping the more representative—but typically less expert—School Planning and Management Team (SPMT) appreciate the gravity of the negative effects that bullying has on the school climate and the students' social, psychological, and intellectual development. The SSST should take the lead in assisting the SPMT to develop strategies and programming to counter bullying in the school. Ideally, the SSST would then work in concert with the SPMT's Staff Development or School Climate subcommittees to implement and/or coordinate the schools efforts to prevent bullying.

CLEVELAND STREET'S RESPONSE: THE STUDENT COURT

One extremely powerful example of a schoolwide approach to bullying and student conflict is the Student Court at the Cleveland Street Elementary School in Orange, New Jersey. What is remarkable about this example is the fact that the students themselves have taken ownership of the Comer Process, to the point of creating a new institution within their school, and have taken responsibility for changing their school and shaping their own development.

Ninety-five percent of the students who attend the Orange schools are African American, but their families hail from many ethnicities, including "indigenous" African Americans and immigrants from Haiti, from other Caribbean countries, and from countries in Africa. Many of the students' families are poor, and student mobility is one of the most difficult problems the schools in Orange must face. The Orange Public Schools entered into a partnership with the School Development Program (SDP) during the 2000–2001 school year to implement systemic reform. This partnership involved the entire district adopting the Comer Process to reorganize and reorient the entire school system toward child and adolescent development in order to carry out their educational mission and school reform mandates.

A problem reported consistently by the Cleveland Street community was the level of conflict between the students at the school. One of the major findings from the school climate data that SDP helped the school collect in 2002 was that the relationships between students were rated as very poor not only by the teachers but also by the students themselves. At Cleveland Street, the data collected with the SDP Student School Climate Survey suggested that while students perceived their relationships with their teachers to be positive (scores slightly exceeded the national average), they rated their relationships with each other as being very poor (average scores on both student interpersonal relationships and order and discipline were far below the national average).

In March 2003, we had an opportunity to interview several of the founders of and current participants in the Student Court, and they described constant fighting between students as a major problem. They also described that a number of their classmates were constantly running in the halls, playing at inappropriate times, joking around and not taking school seriously, and being very disrespectful of both adults and their peers (e.g., talking back, cursing). Many of these students did not respond to the discipline administered by the school administration—in fact, they welcomed it. Eric Brown, a fifth grader at Cleveland described the situation thus:

> When kids were fighting, they would get suspended and go home . . . so they could have free time at home and they don't have to come to school to do their work. And then they would wait for all the kids to get out of school. . . Their parents don't care if they're suspended, and they would just go outside and play.

Many of the students were fed up with their classmates' behavior, and late in the 2001–2002 school year, several members of the school's Student Council and Student Advisory Group came up with an idea for a student court to help solve the problem of all the fighting, name-calling, bullying, and general disrespect present at the school. At first, they discussed their idea with each other, and from the beginning they agreed that they must take responsibility for solving some of their own problems. Even more striking, they recognized that there was usually more than one side to every story and that everyone needed to and should be heard.

The students brought their idea for a student court to Mr. Terrence Brooks, a sixth-grade teacher who serves as the faculty advisor to both the Student Council and Student Advisory Group. Mr. Brooks's classroom is known throughout the school as the "Creative Kingdom," and he is referred to by students, faculty, and staff alike as "Lord Brooks," both for giving to his students and for demanding from them the respect due to royalty. Mr. Brooks and Ms. Janet Walker, a paraprofessional in Mr. Brooks's classroom, guided the students through the process of developing a new institution.

They discussed with the students whether or not a student court was even necessary and the scope of the cases that they thought they should consider. They also asked the students to consider the organization, structure, and procedures they would like to use for the court. The students opted to implement the Student Court and expressed their desire to adopt procedures that mimic as closely as is appropriate those of the legal system. Mr. Brooks took the idea to the school's principal, Mrs. Diana Russ-Harmon, who approved of the court's creation.

In its current form, the presiding judge is Patrice Lewis, a sixth grader who was one of the originators of the idea for the Student Court. Court is in session on Wednesday and Friday each week during a recess period, and cases against students can be brought by anyone in the school community. No one at Cleveland Street Elementary is above the law: On occasion, adults have been brought to court for interacting with students in hostile and negative ways. The school (or plaintiff) and defendant are usually represented by sixth-grade members of the Student Advisory Group, and the jury consists of seven students, typically fifth graders. Students also fulfill the roles of the other court officers, including bailiffs and detectives.

The sentences handed down by the court range from those that might be expected in a school (e.g., cleaning up a classroom, not being allowed to attend a school field trip or social event), to those that are very creative. For example, one young lady who was a bit of a "tomboy" was initially sentenced to "community service" for disrespecting a teacher. She was to monitor the girls' bathroom during lunch, but when she did not show up for her duties, she was brought back to court and subsequently ordered to wear a dress to the next school social function. She reportedly hated wearing the dress, but this young lady, who had been generally unpopular with her peers, did receive a number of compliments from both students and teachers alike, something she reportedly did not hate. She did not disrespect her teacher anymore.

We had an opportunity to observe the court in action, and it was striking how seriously the participating students took their roles. All questions and comments had to be addressed to Judge Patrice, who was addressed by everyone present (including Mr. Brooks and principal Harmon) as "Your Honor." The major case that day involved four third-grade boys who had ignored a teacher's directions to come in from recess. Initially they were "goofing off" and did not take the court proceedings seriously, but from their first interactions with the sixth-grade bailiffs to their questioning before The Honorable Patrice Lewis, both the students and faculty present made it clear that the Court was serious business.

One of the boys was infamous for consistently being in trouble, including stealing from his classmates. When he was accused of stealing again, it was evident by the subsequent comments of his peers that the entire room was fed up with his behavior. I (W. Brown) remember feeling very, very badly for this young man, because no one was advocating for him, and feared that he would continue to be labeled and that his negative behavior would continue. One of the fourth graders, however, Kyleesha Hill, stood before the entire court and said, "We all know that Guillaume (pseudonym) has stolen a bunch of times before, but we don't know for sure that he did it *this* time." The change in Guillaume's demeanor after her statement was instantaneous and dramatic. The restoration of his self-esteem, just from having someone believe in him, was almost palpable. I have rarely been so impressed with any student as I was with Kyleesha, especially given her youth. More than her willingness to presume her classmate's innocence—one of the highest values of our legal system—the understanding, compassion, and courage required to assert her belief and stand up for an unpopular peer in front of an entire classroom was remarkable. Kyleesha was appointed later in the session to represent Guillaume, and I have no doubt that she performed her duties admirably.

Although the students we interviewed described that their sentences worked only some of the time with some of the students and although they expressed a great deal of frustration with the more recalcitrant among them, the faculty and school administration credit the Student Court for vastly improving the climate of the school, an assertion supported by the school climate data collected during the 2002–2003 school year. In the 2001–2002 school year, 60 percent of the staff agreed or strongly agreed with the statement "Students here fight a lot." During the 2002–2003 school year, only 24 percent of the staff agreed with this statement. Similarly, the proportion of the staff that agreed with the statement "Rules are frequently broken by students" dropped from 71 percent in 2001–2002 to 28 percent in 2002–2003. The school's overall score on the Order and Discipline scale increased from 2.61 to 3.65 (the maximum possible score was 5.00) over the two school years. The teachers' perceptions were corroborated by discipline records. The number of suspensions through the end of May 2003 had dropped over 21 percent from the previous year. Despite the fact that the Student Court interventions do not always work, the students agreed that most of the students in the school did not want to go before the Student Court.

Perhaps more important, the student body also reported a greater degree of order and discipline at their school. The overall score increased marginally from 1.71 in 2001–2002 to 1.81 in 2002–2003 (the maximum possible score is 3.00). The students reported, however, that fighting and hurting had decreased significantly. In 2001–2002, 79 percent of the students agreed with the statement "Children at my school fight a lot" and 59 percent agreed with the statement "Children at my school get hurt a lot." In 2002–2003, those proportions had decreased to 55 and 49 percent, respectively. Although the decreases were not as dramatic as those for the teachers, they still represent a tremendous improvement in the students' feelings of personal safety within the school.

The staff of Cleveland Street Elementary credit the Comer Process with helping them to create the environment necessary for students to take on these leadership roles, and the lessons these students are learning from their experiences in their Comer school are numerous and span a variety of areas of development. As one of the students, Ebony Garrison, told us, "I (have) learned that you have to learn how to stay focused, keep yourself disciplined, and have respect for others."

With respect to their individual development, the students are learning about future careers—information that is extremely important for young urban children who may not always have those kinds of experiences in their home. These students are also learning to take initiative and shape their environment, which will be important for their later psychological and social development. They are learning to work with adults and each other in ways that they would not ordinarily do. They are practicing wielding authority responsibly, fairly, and honorably—in this way, they are more developed than many adult leaders in our society. Most important, these students are learning about ethical principles and about the necessity for everyone—both students and adults—to behave in ways that promote positive relationships with each other.

It is a common research finding that students usually know about systematic victimization of the peers within their midst but often do not tell adults in the school, typically for fear of retaliation from or ostracism by their peers. This unwritten rule of silence contributes to escalating cycles of bullying, violence, and victimization within the school. By the same token, students making adults aware of problems as well as stepping in to help solve them, break these cycles of victimization. Using the Comer Process, Cleveland Street has created a climate of trust and communication, where students not only feel permitted, but actually encouraged to do something about maltreatment within the school. If the purpose of the Comer Process is to create fertile ground for development, the students of Cleveland Street Elementary are definitely bearing fruit.

PUTTING THE COMER PROCESS INTO ACTION TO ADDRESS BULLYING

In a 1981 column for the magazine *Parents*, Dr. Comer wrote,

> Staff and school authorities should take any vicious behavior seriously, stepping in where necessary to prevent psychological or physical damage to a victimized youngster, using punishment where appropriate, and, most important, helping students learn more mature ways of handling their fears and anxieties. (p. 126)

His words are no less true today than when he wrote them, and they are even more important now. Schools, however, can attempt to treat these problems reactively—treating incidents of school violence as isolated problems and dealing with them as they occur—or they can use a proactive and preventative approach by enhancing the climate of the school to create an environment or climate of trust and communication between all the members of the school community. In this kind of environment, students will learn to work well with school adults and will learn to take responsibility for their own development and for the welfare of others around them. It is precisely these lessons that would contribute to decreasing the tragic impact of bullying and other forms of aggression and violence at our schools.

From its inception, the Comer Process has focused on the importance of adequate and healthy relationships within the school as the foundation for healthy development and all productive educational activity. While a great deal of day-to-day attention is paid to the structural components and organizational functions of the Comer Process, it is critical to remember that the fundamental purpose of the three guiding principles, the three teams, and the three operations is to strengthen and enhance the quality of the tapestry of relationships within the school *in order to promote the students' development*. The SSST has a unique and important role in identifying and promoting the developmental needs of the students, but enhancing child and adolescent development is the primary and fundamental task of every adult in the school—regardless of their position, duty, or function.

REFERENCE

Comer, J. P. (1981, October). Scapegoating and vicious behavior. *Parents, 56*, 126.

AUTHORS' NOTE: The authors would like to express their thanks to the students of Cleveland Street Elementary School, and especially Eric Brown (sixth grade), Rana Campbell (sixth grade), Brionna Garrison (second grade), Ebony Garrison (sixth grade), Jasmine Larmond (sixth grade), Alyssa Marshall (sixth grade), and Kamielah Tyler (fifth grade) for participating in the student focus group.

14

Letters From an Experienced Facilitator

Youth Guidance Comer SDP Team

As a change agent based in a school or cluster of schools, the Comer facilitator provides the assigned school with leadership in implementing the Comer Process; coordinates School Development Program (SDP) training in conjunction with the school's Staff Development Subcommittee; provides the SDP teams, administration, and school staff with technical assistance in SDP program implementation and school reform; promotes the use of the three guiding principles (no-fault, collaboration, consensus) throughout the school community; assists the school in the collection of data and promotes the implementation of a data-driven change process; informs the school community of research-based practices; encourages the school to relate knowledge of child and youth development to student learning; works with the district and SDP Implementation Coordinator to optimize school resources; promotes family involvement; and monitors SDP program implementation. Facilitators from Chicago's Youth Guidance, a private social service agency founded in 1924, guide SDP implementation in Chicago schools. In this chapter, the facilitators present their hard-earned wisdom in the form of letters from a consummate facilitator, first to parents and then to a novice facilitator just beginning her journey.

A LETTER TO PARENTS: INITIATING RELATIONSHIPS WITH PARENTS AND FAMILIES

Dear Parents and Guardians,

I am so happy to be involved with you and your child's school. I will be available in the school one day a week, and I want to be really involved with parents. The primary reason that I am writing this letter is to introduce myself to you—and to start building a relationship between us. As the school's new facilitator of the Comer Process, I want to know you personally as well as professionally so that we can develop a relationship. I want to be able to connect you with your children.

For our first parent meeting next week, we have many options: We could talk about how, as parents, we can make sure that our children are sent off to school physically fit, with a good breakfast, emotionally secure, with a hug, a kiss, and an "I love you"—knowing that they need to make good decisions and not stray. We could brainstorm about possible workshops we could have. We could do a workshop on the Comer Process and each of the developmental pathways, for example. At workshops that I run, parents share their ideas because I like to learn from parents. You are the expert on your child. We'll share information because we're all learning this ongoing process of parenting.

The facilitator is the "go-to" person for questions about "What is this Comer Process?" The Comer Process is based on an understanding of the developmental needs of children. Let's set up parent meetings. It would be terrific to have a core group of parents who meet on a weekly or monthly basis to talk about how the school community may best promote the learning and development of all the children in the school.

Let's spend some time talking about whether the school is meeting your needs. Do you feel welcome in the school? Have you ever attended any of the school's meetings or open houses? Have you ever visited your child's teacher? Have you ever gotten a call for any reason other than that your child has misbehaved?

As the school's facilitator of the Comer Process, my role is to help you see that *you* are the process. School communities sometimes have the perception that a new program, whatever it is, will be the magical solution to their problems. They don't see the connection between what they have to do to make it work and the expertise that the outside program designers bring. You're going to have to work to make the Comer Process happen in your school. My role as facilitator is to provide the training and coaching. Your role is to make it work in the long term.

I would like you to feel that I am open and receptive, that you can talk to me, that I'm understanding, and that I'm on everybody's side. I really am on everybody's side. I'm on the parent's side, I'm on the teacher's side, I'm on the principal's side, and I'm on the children's side. I'm on everybody's side and I'm listening. I will help you to see issues from all angles: How would you feel if you were the principal or the teacher and this happened? I will not be caught up in people games. I promise that whatever you tell me in confidence will remain between the two of us. I am in the school as a neutral person. My main focus is on what is best for the children— and I will try hard to stay focused.

Let's start building a relationship between us. Call me. I'm available. I will call on you.

Take care,

A LETTER TO A NEW FACILITATOR: BECOMING A RESOURCE TO THE SCHOOL COMMUNITY

Dear Michelle,

I am so pleased that you decided to join our team as a facilitator. You asked me what it will take for you to facilitate a school community the way I do. I suggest that I e-mail different ideas to you and you ask me questions.

Within the school community, I'm the coach and the reminder person (the person who knows the calendar and gets the agendas out and makes sure that things are copied and distributed). The school community can rely on me to challenge people to resolve conflicts, create a no-fault environment, and model academic excellence. Sometimes I model academic excellence simply by remaining hopeful about a student. Facilitators often hear teachers recite a litany of problems about a child. Sometimes teachers just want to be agreed with. At those times, they may feel that we are like a frustrating superego because we always say, "No, you can make this work. This child can learn, and will learn, and we will find a way to make that happen. Let's figure this out together."

I am also the production assistant. I am the behind-the-scenes person who helps the school community use the Comer Process. When I see people about to handle an issue in the old, traditional way, I help them see that they could handle the issue even more effectively if they use the School Planning and Management Team or a committee that was formed. As the behind-the-scenes person, I am a resource to the school community. I tell teachers, "I'm not here monitoring or looking over your shoulder. I'm here to help facilitate your role as a teacher and support you in your efforts to enhance the skills of the students. You can count on my confidentiality and discretion."

Take care,

A LETTER TO A NEW FACILITATOR: ESTABLISHING EFFECTIVE RELATIONSHIPS WITH PEOPLE IN THE SCHOOL

Dear Michelle,

I am glad that you find my reflections helpful to you as you begin preparing to take on the role of the facilitator. You had asked me about establishing relationships with people in the school.

I am not going to be pulled into the school's hidden agendas. That's not my role. My role is to help address those hidden agendas. Sometimes it means bringing them out into the open, putting them on the table, stirring things up, causing some chaos in this school. I will bring up old issues that have festered under the surface for a long time—and confront them. I am no use to the school community if I get caught up in their games. I am no use to the school if I'm not honest. I am no use if I perceive things going on that are detrimental to children and I do not say anything out loud. But before I can do that, I need to establish personal relationships with each and every person in the school.

And my relationships are going to be different. My relationship with the principal is going to be different from my relationship with a parent. And that is because the principal has a different role than a parent. I tell people, "You may see me more often with the principal, but that does not mean that I hold you in any less esteem. And you may see me with a weaker teacher more often, but that doesn't mean that I'm not paying attention to your needs. I'm usually where I need to be at that moment. Even though you might not be aware of the reasons why I'm there at that particular teacher's classroom or that particular meeting, I'm aware. Sometimes it's for the betterment of all the children in the school that I'm there." Sometimes I may remain quiet at a meeting, and after the meeting I sit with the principal and I say, "Hey—let's talk about this meeting. We know that there are things that should be done and that should not be done at meetings, and your behavior today was so totally out of line." Now, people might not see that. They might not see me having this conversation with the principal. Yet they will see the results.

Take care,

A LETTER TO A NEW FACILITATOR: MAINTAINING CLEAR AND TRUSTWORTHY COMMUNICATIONS

Dear Michelle,

You asked about the facilitator's job in providing feedback to people in the school.

I have said to school communities, "I am not here to make you feel incompetent. I am here to give you feedback, and this is what I am observing. . . ." I provide unsolicited advice: I tell them, "Even though it has not occurred to you to ask me my opinion on this topic, I am freely going to share my expertise with you. I'm going to let you know what I think."

Most important, my experience has taught me that there first needs to be a foundation of trust between people in order for the feedback process to work. I have found that it is critical for me to publicly apologize when I've made a mistake. In this way, I model that I reflect on my actions and internally go through the feedback process that I advocate. I've said at meetings, "Listen: I was wrong in how I said that"; "I was wrong, and I shouldn't have said that at a public meeting."

There is another point I want to make about how I establish trust with school communities. People cannot establish trust with one another if they fail in communicating effectively. I tell people up front that I cannot read minds. Sometimes people will be vague during conversations. They'll talk around a topic instead of talking directly. They'll leave out necessary information. They'll assume I know more than I actually do. I'll leave a few books for you in the office on communication excellence. I've had to teach people how to listen actively and establish rapport. Take time when you are having conversations with people in your schools to clarify what they are really trying to say underneath all the verbiage. Don't respond until you feel that you have a clear sense of what the other person hopes to achieve by communicating with you. Keep in mind that you may have to teach communication skills to the other person before he or she truly understands what you want to convey.

Take care,

15

The Comer Facilitator and Teaming Skills for Meetings

Yale School Development Program Staff

An old saying holds that the "Jack of all trades" is "master of none," but this is not the case for Comer facilitators. These exemplars of the Comer Process embody all of SDP's principles and skills, and they also teach and support all school and district SDP teams. Their goal is to help adults and children become facilitators themselves, working together effectively while planning and managing change in the best interests of the students. This chapter reviews facilitators' responsibilities, skills, and strategies and offers many guidelines for most effective practices.

IT TAKES A UNIQUE PERSON TO CHANGE A WHOLE SCHOOL

In talking with Comer facilitators, it is clear that the role is highly ambiguous. In many ways, the Comer facilitator role is unique. It is distinctive because of what it is not—not just another pair of hands, not just a staff developer, not just technical assistance, not just a personal mediator. Yet all of these parts come into play at one time or another. Rather than say, "A Comer facilitator is everything" (however true that might be), it is important to begin to describe what a Comer facilitator is.

The Comer facilitator is a change agent—an individual inside or outside the school whose defined role is to provide support, technical assistance, and training in the ongoing process of school improvement. The facilitator challenges the usual way of doing things, energizes the school community to come to terms with its problems, and draws attention to the need for change. A change agent has the ability to

- motivate and guide others to see things in different ways
- achieve results through working with others and seeing projects through to completion
- understand the depth and breadth of how schools are transformed
- create an environment that fosters change, risk-taking, and accountability
- research contemporary issues, policies, and practices in educational reform as well as child, youth, and adult development

As a coach, the facilitator shows the school community how to recognize and define needs, analyze problems and set goals, and obtain resources. The facilitator has the ability to

- work effectively with others regardless of level, status, or ethnic background
- organize the school and Comer teams in ways that reflect team planning, problem solving, and effective decision making
- increase the quality and level of parent participation
- develop rapport and trust among colleagues, staff, administration, and community
- develop a sense of unity and common purpose among the school community
- respect and value the opinions of others
- involve social agencies and other community services in the life of the school
- provide parents with opportunities to enhance their own development and the development of their children
- manage conflict

Our assumption at SDP is that all of the adults become leaders in some way. If we look at the facilitator as a leader, we see a specific type of leadership, but there are other ways of leading. The dimensions of leadership chart shown in Figure 15.1 can help both facilitators and principals to reflect on their leadership roles.

All facilitators coordinate the implementation of the Comer Process. Facilitators literally embody the Comer Process and mind-set. They demonstrate flexibility and expertise in change management. Moreover, they relate knowledge of child and youth development to student learning. They insist that all decisions are made in the best interests of children.

There are different models of facilitation within the SDP network. In some SDP districts, facilitators are employees of the school district and are based at the schools; a Comer Action Team or districtwide facilitator is based at the school district central office. In other districts, facilitators are based at a private social service agency or a nearby university.

A Comer facilitator's goal is to encourage others to become their own facilitators so that problems are solved collaboratively and all decisions are made in the best interests of children. As the mind-set of the Comer Process infuses the school community, people's capacity for self-renewal increases and they feel empowered by change to reach their ultimate goals for the school.

Figure 15.1 Dimensions of leadership in education

The purpose of this chart is to consider four dimensions of the leadership role. A mistake that leaders can make is to view leadership one dimensionally. Principals, while they are primarily administrators or managers, will see that they have a major responsibility to facilitate relationships. Facilitators will find that they need to develop the dimensions of manager, administrator, and visionary.

Mature leaders understand that all four dimensions of leadership are equally important. Each of the dimensions needs to be differentiated and articulated. Each adds complexity and requires more personal and professional development. The highly functioning leader develops all four types of leadership in order to use each dimension appropriately and effectively.

	The leader as facilitator	The leader as manager	The leader as administrator	The leader as visionary
Focus	When leading in this way, the individual's focus is on promoting a sense of belonging, healthy relationships, and connections within the organization.	When leading in this way, the individual fosters the will of the organization and encourages commitment. The focus is on responsibility, mastery, and assessing risk.	When leading in this way, the individual encourages coherence within the organization. The focus is on establishing and maintaining a well-functioning bureaucracy.	When leading in this way, the individual's focus is on coaching in order to foster confluence (integration) even while promoting individuality and freedom.
Orientation	People and process oriented. When leading in this way, the individual looks for connections among people, creates opportunities for collaboration, and tries to foster community.	Task oriented. When leading in this way, the individual looks for connections among events and accomplishments. Opportunities for change are created. The individual tries to foster responsibility by setting goals and objectives.	Achievement oriented. When leading in this way, the individual looks for connections among fragments (parts). Opportunities are created for consensus decision making. The individual tries to foster structure, order, safety, trust, and boundaries.	Vision oriented. When leading in this way, the individual looks for connections among ideas. Opportunities are created for reflection, autonomy, and no-fault problem solving. The individual tries to foster insight, creativity, and knowledge.

(Continued)

Figure 15.1 (Continued)

	The leader as facilitator	The leader as manager	The leader as administrator	The leader as visionary
Aim	The work is about influencing and integrating policies and people.	The work is about taking action.	The work is about setting policies, procedures, and controls.	The work is about guiding, differentiating, and setting direction.
Actions	Attends to the people issues of the organization. Emphasis on feeling and being.	Attends to internal issues within the organization. Emphasis on doing.	Attends to external factors that impact the well-functioning of the organization. Emphasis on planning.	Attends to internal and external frameworks of the organization. Emphasis on thinking.
Outcomes	Desire to belong and feel valued.	Desire to have a special impact on the world.	Desire to feel safe and in control.	Desire for inner discovery and finding out about the world.

SOURCE: J. Patrick Howley, personal communication, 2004.

The following are among the duties and responsibilities of a Comer facilitator:

- Provide the assigned school with leadership in implementing the Comer Process.
- Coordinate Comer training and other staff and parent staff development in conjunction with the Staff Development Subcommittee.
- Provide the school staff, teams, and administration with technical assistance in program implementation and school reform.
- Assist all the teams and subcommittees in using the three guiding principles (consensus, collaboration, and no-fault) when making decisions.
- Assist the school in the collection and use of student assessment and program evaluation data.
- Provide information on promising initiatives and practices (e.g., effective teaching).
- Assist the school in designing and implementing school improvement strategies that support student learning and development.
- Assist the School Planning and Management Team (SPMT) in designing an inclusive process for updating the Comprehensive School Plan and in using that plan to guide the work of the school.
- Work with the school district and other leadership groups to optimize school resources.
- Attend as many meetings as possible of the three teams, subcommittees, and grade levels to promote the application of school and team resources in the service of student learning and development.
- Work with the parents and volunteers.
- Monitor School Development Program (SDP) implementation.

The Comer facilitator is self-directed. This means he or she has the ability to systematically structure tasks and plans; work with teams to establish goals, set objectives, and follow-up on assigned tasks; complete tasks with efficiency; work independently with little direction or supervision; and assume responsibility for personal and professional growth.

A Comer facilitator uses many skills when working with groups to help them solve problems. A facilitator is able to

- listen diagnostically
- summarize information without injecting personal bias
- record certain vignettes, video clips, and other selections for future use
- organize by anticipating what needs to be done ahead of time
- minimize any threats that others may pose to group members
- demonstrate flexibility
- display caring
- motivate by creating an atmosphere that fosters self-confidence, acceptance, openness, and trust
- empathize by identifying with the group's point of view
- manage by giving clear directions
- pace the group by keeping things moving while maintaining sensitivity to the energy level of the group
- resolve conflict
- support ideas
- display mutuality by recognizing shared interests, experiences, values, and standards as a basis of establishing relationships
- handle resistance without becoming defensive
- demonstrate timing by probing and making suggestions when the group is ready to respond
- take risks and explore new ideas
- bring closure through debriefing and other techniques
- process a group by leading them in a series of interrelated activities toward a specific goal
- recognize and appreciate contributions of individuals or the group

The Comer Process deals with group and individual change. Changing traditions, group norms, and behavior is a slow process. These structures involve emotions, which are most difficult and time-consuming to change. However, once the changes are adopted, they are long lasting.

IF YOU ARE A FACILITATOR IN A NEW SDP SCHOOL COMMUNITY

School and Community Orientation

- Gain a working knowledge of the school and community. Become aware of all feeder patterns and the communities that represent the school. Investigate the level of parent involvement in the school's decision making.

- Get a sense of the values, norms, and leadership patterns that set the climate of the school. Get a feel for the environment and people who can assist in creating the conditions necessary for change.

- Become a positive coach and encourage others to higher levels of effectiveness.

- Discuss the need for school improvement with students, staff, and parents. Create a vision for the kind of change that is needed to improve the climate, curriculum, student activities, and family involvement.

- Participate in a networking and planning meeting with the Comer leadership teams in your district or other nearby schools that are implementing the Comer Process.

- Introduce the Comer Process to administrators, teachers, support staff, parents, community members, students, and unions.

- Establish a Comer resource and reference area within the school.

- Develop a school profile that includes student demographic and achievement data for at least the previous five years.

The School Planning and Management Team

- Help establish the SPMT. Emphasize representation of the total school community of parents, teachers, students, administrators, and support staff. When figuring out which instructional staff members should sit on the SPMT, consider such factors as subject area specialties, ethnic backgrounds, and the fact that some teachers have a great deal of experience and others are new.

- Meet with the principal and chair to plan the SPMT agenda.

- Distribute the SPMT agenda to the whole staff.

- Working with the principal and chair, convene the first SPMT and establish meeting guidelines.

- Distribute the minutes of the meeting to the whole staff.

- Establish subcommittees.

- Develop and post a schoolwide calendar in collaboration with the Public Relations Subcommittee (or whatever group fulfills this function).

- Conduct training sessions in collaboration with the Professional Development Subcommittee on selected topics.

- Provide the entire school with the Comprehensive School Plan. Prepare and distribute an abbreviated version to the families.

The Student and Staff Support Team

- Help establish the team by coordinating schedules of an administrator, the school psychologist, school social worker, school counselor, a special education teacher, school nurse, and other professional staff.

- Conduct training sessions on selected topics.

- Help the team design a system for maintaining a log of students served. It should include a status assessment that is kept current for each of those students.

- Help the team prepare an orientation for the school staff that explains the team's role, function, and referral process.

- Encourage the team to compile a directory of community organizations and agencies.

The Parent Team

- Conduct meetings with the current parent group to explain the Comer Process and select representatives to serve on the Parent Team.

- Develop and distribute a survey to the families in order to identify topics for future family workshops.

- Convene the Parent Team and guide the process of selecting representatives to the SPMT.

- Assist the principal and chair in the development of the Parent Team agenda.

- Distribute minutes of the meetings to the school community.

IF YOU ARE NEW TO AN SDP SCHOOL

If you are new to a school that is already an SDP school, set up a meeting with the principal. Meet with the whole school staff to review your role and responsibilities as well as the goals of SDP. Make sure you have an in-depth understanding of your school.

- Read the Comprehensive School Plan.
- Locate all data relative to the school.
- Know the whole staff, parent and community leaders, system people working with your school, School Board members, etc.
- Obtain a copy of the calendars of the school and school district. These will help you think globally as teams plan for events. Do the proposed events conflict with already scheduled events of other schools in the neighborhood?
- Obtain a list of SPMT, SSST, and Parent Team members and a schedule of when the teams meet.
- Obtain a copy of the staff and parent handbook.

Remember that new facilitators must establish themselves as likeable, credible, and trustworthy. Engage in open and supportive communication. Clarify expectations. Occasionally patrol the halls. Help with bus or cafeteria duty. Occasionally mentor small groups of students. Arrive at school early to meet and greet incoming staff and students. (Be in the halls!)

In conjunction with the Staff Development Subcommittee, develop a portfolio of everyone who has been trained in the Comer Process and all other initiatives. How have they used the training they received? How can you support their growth? Would it help to hold meetings of those who have received Comer training to hear their perspectives on what should happen next? Constantly assess where the school is and what they need to fully implement the Comer Process. Before people from your school attend staff development activities outside the school, brief them on the expectations of the Staff Development Subcommittee. Work with the SPMT to select representative staff and parents to attend. The following questions may guide your thinking:

- Are they capable and willing to train others on what they learn?
- Will they be effective in their presentation of new material?
- Are they influential and respected by others in the school?
- Will they be here next year?
- Is the perception that the same people in your school are always sent to everything? Have you made sure to select people of different grade levels, ethnicities, genders, and levels of experience?

Attend different events in the school. Be seen as willing to help out—"get down and dirty." Model the behaviors you want from others. For example, at parent events, model welcoming behaviors. Don't be seen sitting with the same group each time. Arrive early to events to help out (but don't do all the work). When you volunteer to assist with projects, keep this in mind: Is this the best way I can support the school at this time? Will my participation enable people to see a good model of "whatever it takes" to stay focused on the students' development? Will this bring the school closer to faithfully replicating the Comer Process? See Figure 15.2 for tips on deepening implementation of the Comer Process in your school.

IN A NEW SCHOOL COMMUNITY AND IN A VETERAN SDP SCHOOL COMMUNITY: AFTER THE INITIAL STEPS

Contact the media specialist or other key influential people to collaboratively develop a Comer SDP Corner or an instructional corner with books and articles about the Comer Process. Include all of Dr. Comer's books and articles. Consider other information that parents may need: child development, higher-level thinking, state testing, cooperative learning, and so on. Distribute Comer brochures or information sheets at all events and to new parents and families when they register.

Assist in developing the school's volunteer program. This may mean having the SPMT and staff determine what it is they want from volunteers. Encourage the

Figure 15.2 Ten easy ways to deepen the implementation of the Comer School Development Program in your school

1. Make certain that Comer SDP is described in your school improvement plan, faculty/staff handbook, school brochure, parent handbook, and student planner as your model for comprehensive school reform.

2. Develop a Comer Corner in your school media center.

3. Include a section for Comer SDP highlights in your school newsletter.

4. Have a Comer SDP teachable moment at every SPMT, SSST, PTA/PTSA/PTO, and SGA meeting.

5. Build a critical mass of staff and parents/families who have knowledge about Comer SDP by sending committed individuals and/or teams to countywide and national Comer SDP training events, as well as scheduling Comer SDP training on professional development days. Charge all training participants with returning to train others.

6. Encourage teachers to use a developmental pathways classroom lesson plan form for all curricular areas.

7. Distribute Guiding Principles tents to be placed on all tables at all staff meetings and in all classrooms.

8. Make certain that the Comer SDP Schoolhouse posters are posted in all major hallways in your building and that a mini Comer SDP Schoolhouse poster is hanging in every classroom.

9. Give each student a Guiding Principles palm-size card after a Comer-in-the-Classroom lesson.

10. Give each parent/community/business partner visitor a Comer SDP brochure or Comer SDP information page.

SOURCE: Created by Jennifer Gordon, Topeka, and modified by Sheila Jackson. Courtesy of Prince George's County Public Schools, Maryland.

distribution of information sheets or applications at Back-to-School Night. Help the Adult Development and Training Subcommittee set up a training program for volunteers. Make phone calls to help out. Help staff to understand that follow-up is critical once a person has offered to volunteer.

Meet with new teachers to educate them about SDP. Meet with the executive board of the school's parent organization (PTA/PTSA/PTO). Familiarize them with SDP. Remind them to talk about the SPMT at every meeting.

Join a professional organization. Read journals on your own. Attend workshops and inservice training that will support your own understanding of curriculum, instruction, child and youth development, and group dynamics. At the same time, be certain that you don't become the only one to attend Comer events. Spread the wealth. Encourage others to take the lead.

Stay visible in your school. Go to classrooms. Enter every classroom at least once a year to talk about the Comer Process with the students. Ask classroom teachers to remain in the room so they hear about the Comer Process from a new perspective. Save your lesson plans to share with other facilitators.

Maintain accurate records for documentation. How will you know that you are making a difference? Summarize evaluations from inservice events and share them with the teams. Keep a school data profile and update it every year. Ask the staff to provide you with feedback (see Figure 15.3).

Figure 15.3 Asking school staff to provide feedback

Comerandum

To: School Staff and Parent Team
From: Your Comer facilitator
Re: The Comer SDP Facilitator Assessment

Assessment and modification is an integral part of what we all do. I would appreciate your assistance in completing this assessment so I may evaluate my services and role in our school and in the implementation of the Comer Process.

Thank you for taking the time to do this.

Year_____

School _____ **Facilitator** _____

TO WHAT EXTENT DOES THE COMER FACILITATOR:

	Don't Know	To a Limited Degree	To a Moderate Degree	To a High Degree
Interact with the instructional staff	1	2	3	4
Interact with noninstructional support staff	1	2	3	4
Interact with parents/families and other community members	1	2	3	4
Interact with your school administrator(s)	1	2	3	4
Help out when special needs arise	1	2	3	4
Interact with students/work in classrooms	1	2	3	4
Act as a resource for information and research	1	2	3	4
Promote collaboration in the school	1	2	3	4

TO WHAT EXTENT HAS THE COMER FACILITATOR ASSISTED THE SCHOOL
(AND/OR TEAMS) IN FOCUSING ON:

	Don't Know	To a Limited Degree	To a Moderate Degree	To a High Degree
Instructional or curriculum issues	1	2	3	4
Child or adolescent growth and development	1	2	3	4
Effective teaming	1	2	3	4
Effective problem solving	1	2	3	4
Adult relationships	1	2	3	4
Multicultural awareness and sensitivity	1	2	3	4
Students' social/interpersonal skills	1	2	3	4
School improvement plan (developing, monitoring, assessing)	1	2	3	4

TO WHAT EXTENT DOES THE COMER FACILITATOR:

	Don't Know	To a Limited Degree	To a Moderate Degree	To a High Degree
Inspire trust	1	2	3	4
Participate as a part of your staff	1	2	3	4
Make an effort to be helpful	1	2	3	4
Make an effort to be available or "visible"	1	2	3	4
Attend SSST meetings	1	2	3	4
Attend SPMT meetings	1	2	3	4
Attend Parent Team meetings	1	2	3	4

(Continued)

Figure 15.3 (Continued)

Attend subcommittee meetings	1	2	3	4
Model all the principles and practices of the Comer Process	1	2	3	4

Role of the facilitator is to assist school staff, students, and the community in infusing the Comer philosophy, principles, and practices into the school improvement planning process as well as into the day-to-day operations of the school. As a change agent, the facilitator works closely with administrators, teachers, students, support staff, and parents/families to build and model strong relationships that support and nurture change. The facilitator acts as a coach to aid the key stakeholders in the school in creating well-functioning teams that facilitate communication and foster strong academic and social support for students. The role is a complex one and unique in each school.

DIRECTIONS: Please provide feedback to your school's facilitator with regard to the items above. In the space below, please briefly describe SPECIFIC ways your facilitator assisted you this year.

Have a personal support system. When you are dealing with issues and/or people who are resistant or frustrated, it can be a lonely job. Stay objective with the people at your school. Use your support system for venting, reflecting, and problem solving. Remember that you are human and you are not alone in the challenges you face.

Figure 15.4 represents designs of buttons that were created to be a visual/concrete reminder of several important practices within SDP. They are often worn as a reminder to the person wearing them. They have also become a symbol of what is important to parents and staff working together in schools to make a difference for all children. They are also a great "talk piece" when you are out and about and others stop and ask you the meaning of the buttons.

SOME TIPS

- Keep your calendar updated and use it at every meeting.
- Be prompt or early to meetings so you can make sure everything is set up correctly.
- Involve others in all that you do.
- Listen and stay focused.
- Accept failure as an opportunity to learn.

Figure 15.4 Facilitator buttons: No-fault, Modeling Matters

- Function with a purpose—write lesson plans daily.
- Set realistic and concrete goals for yourself.
- Don't take personally everything that happens around you.
- Believe in yourself and the process.
- Seek advice, listen, and learn from others.
- Understand and follow the system's rules, regulations, and policies.
- Be an excellent presenter. Rehearse. Practice with the equipment. If need be, get help from others on visuals, but keep to as high a technical and educational standard as possible. Ask others for feedback.
- Read all of Dr. Comer's books and articles.
- Believe it: Modeling does matter.

Haynes, Ben-Avie, Squires, Howley, Negron, and Corbin (1996) explain that the Comer facilitator has multiple roles (p. 56):

- *Organizational development facilitation on the change process.* A facilitator of a team meeting is part of the team and helps both tasks and processes to move forward. The facilitator must listen, give feedback, clarify issues, and ask questions well, ensuring a balance of participation and, most important, modeling consensus, collaboration, and no-fault.
- *Process consultant for team meetings.* A process consultant is not part of the team but observes the dynamics of the meeting. The focus is exclusively on process and the goal is to give feedback so the team can better understand its own process.
- *Coach.* A coach helps either a team or an individual become better at a particular skill. A Comer facilitator may coach a principal on more collaborative

behaviors, coach a team on giving feedback, and coach a teacher on how to see his or her students more in terms of their development than in terms of behavior or grades.

- *"Whatever it takes."* A key element of good facilitation is the development of strong relationships. Since schools are such busy places, Comer facilitators often pitch in to do the task at hand.

REFERENCE

Haynes, N. M., Ben-Avie, M., Squires, D., Howley, J. P., Negron, E., & Corbin, J. (1996). It takes a whole village. In J. P. Comer, N. M. Haynes, E. Joyner, & M. Ben-Avie (Eds.), *Rallying the whole village: The Comer Process for reforming education* (pp. 42–71). New York: Teachers College Press.

16

Facilitators Model Communication Excellence

Trudy Raschkind Steinfeld and Michael Ben-Avie

The criteria and beliefs that people hold—consciously and unconsciously—are powerful motivators behind their ability to work well on teams. Facilitators not only help uncover these often hidden motivators, but they also teach team members to express them in more positive ways. This commentary discusses the importance of learning and respecting one's own and other people's criteria and illustrates the point with case vignettes.

Often, when schools take on the Comer Process there is already "a lot of water under the bridge" in some groups—for example, a history of bitter battles over votes and decision making. Having a facilitator to train group members allows people to slow down and get to know one another in a different way. One of the important things to know about other people is what they feel motivates them (as opposed to what you assume motivates them).

MOTIVATORS MAY BE POSITIVE OR NEGATIVE

In large part, people are motivated to participate in or to avoid any particular discussion or project by the criteria and beliefs they hold (Bateson, 1972/2000; Dilts,

1999; Gordon & Dawes, 2004; O'Connor & Seymour, 1990). Criteria are the concepts (e.g., honesty, dissent) and internal states (e.g., satisfaction, discomfort) that people consider to be significantly positive or negative. They motivate us to move toward or away from any given situation because they are the standards against which we measure whether we are getting or are likely to get our personal outcomes.

A person who believes "easiness" to be an important criterion to go toward will probably avoid situations that seem too difficult. A person who believes "struggle" to be an important criterion to go toward will probably disengage from situations that seem too easy. A person who believes "excitement" to be an important criterion to move away from may continually try to avoid conflict. A person who believes "boredom" to be an important criterion to move away from may try to stir things up. Now imagine all these people trying to work together on the same team!

Some of these criteria are evident in the words people use, and some are evident in their behavior. Facilitators help group members to notice each other's key words and phrases and significant behaviors, and to become curious about the positive motivators that may be hidden behind even negative expressions. Let's consider two case studies.

CASE 16.1: WHAT EXCELLENCE AND HARD WORK LOOK LIKE

In the first case, a consensus process was being attempted to plan ways of bringing parents into the classroom. One third-grade teacher was adamantly refusing to agree. She kept repeating that the parents always were "trouble." Through supportive statements and thoughtful questioning, the facilitator slowed things down so the teacher could explore her own motivations. With strong emotion, she described herself as a perfectionist who felt that she couldn't always live up to the standards set by other teachers on her grade, even though she worked very hard, and she feared gossip and comparisons by the parents.

Some of her important motivators were her own excellence (a "toward" criterion), caring about her students (toward), being talked about and compared (an "away from" criterion), trouble (away from), confusion (away from), hard work (toward), doing it all by herself (toward), and perseverance (toward). The obvious caring and support she received from her fellow group members helped her to agree to think about allowing parents into her classroom.

At the next meeting, the facilitator led a team-building exercise that had parents and teachers list on the reverse of their name badge three qualities they admired in themselves and discuss one of them with a partner. The teacher was paired with a mother she had previously privately labeled as being "too young to know anything yet." The mother did not speak English and the teacher did not speak Spanish, so an interpreter translated every comment.

The teacher learned that the mother had walked, barefoot, for many months to get into the United States from a war zone in Central America in order to make a better life for her child. The mother said that she had been fearful at first but had come to realize that she was strong and therefore would have enough courage to learn even something as hard as English. The teacher burst into tears and embraced her. Even though their personal situations were very different, their criteria matched in so many ways that it would have been almost impossible for them not to become allies.

The teacher allowed parents into her classroom.

CASE 16.2: ONE PERSON'S ARGUMENT IS ANOTHER PERSON'S DISCUSSION

In another case, a facilitator discovered by accident that the most negative person on a team was perfectly happy to be in agreement as long as someone else was fulfilling the role of arguer! This team member had a (probably unconscious) need for a certain amount of heated, rapid, finger-pointing, back-and-forth "discussion" before feeling satisfied that all avenues had been explored. Satisfaction was a highly valued criterion for her, and she had a belief that argument was prerequisite for satisfaction. That went a long way toward explaining why she persisted in offering reasons why every suggestion wouldn't work, even though everyone else in the room was openly annoyed with her behavior.

RECOGNIZING AND WORKING WITH PEOPLE'S CRITERIA

When people are attempting to meet their most important criteria, they may very well disregard other people's cues, such as scowls, pencil tapping, attempts to interrupt them, and so on. Training in the skills of the consensus process not only helps people to notice these important cues, but it helps them to discover and respect their own and each other's motivators. In retrospect, group members' past behaviors become easier to understand, making it possible for people to develop new attitudes about one another.

One way to deal with the behaviors of a person like the one described in Case 16.2 is for the facilitator to speak with her privately, helping to unpackage her criteria (and learning more about her positive intentions in the process). Then the facilitator can help her to mentally rehearse and actually practice other ways to achieve satisfaction during a team meeting. At that point it will be possible for her to literally downgrade the relative importance of her old behaviors so that she is more likely to demonstrate the new ones. The facilitator can also have one-on-one conversations with other team members to discover (1) the positive motivations underlying their current reactions to the "difficult" team member, and (2) alternative attitudes and behaviors they can develop that would lead to different outcomes for the group.

It helps to express criteria in positive terms. For example, if a teacher says, "I don't want to have trouble with these parents in my classroom," the facilitator can ask, "What's important about not having trouble? What does that do *for* you?" or "When you're not having trouble with the parents in your classroom, what will your experience be like then?" A typical response might be, "Then things will go smoothly." So "smoothness" is one positive way to express this criterion. Further conversation with the same person might produce other descriptions, such as "professional," "orderly," and "happy," each of which is also a positive way—for that person—of expressing "no trouble."

People usually hold different criteria for different situations. Over time, though, a well-functioning group can notice which criteria tend to come up again and again or to be expressed with special emphasis of some sort (perhaps a change in voice tone or tempo or underscored by certain postures or gestures). *Criteria emphasized in this way are the most highly valued criteria, and they must be understood according to that person's definition, respected, and accommodated in a way the person recognizes if he or she is to remain engaged.* Expressed in positive terms, these criteria can become part of a criteria checklist, which can help the group make sure the topics under discussion and the form of the discussion can engage as many members as possible with the greatest motivation.

MOTIVATING CRITERIA FOR THE COMER PROCESS

It is worth noting that criteria are not the sole property of adults. Every student, no matter how young, is also motivated toward and away from discussion and action by his or her criteria. Having Comer-in-the-Classroom permits educators to bring their understanding of motivation directly to the students.

One of the great benefits of the Comer Process is that the most highly valued criteria for any group and for any group member are set by Dr. Comer himself: All decisions must be in the best interests of children, and there are six developmental pathways whose conditions must be met. It is very helpful to have the Comer Process as the higher authority to which one can point when individual criteria seem to be getting in the way of achieving consensus. Another great benefit of the Comer Process is that SDP-trained facilitators work in school districts and schools to help all members of the school community manage and embrace change.

REFERENCES

Bateson, G. (1972/2000). *Steps to an ecology of mind.* Chicago: University of Chicago Press.

Dilts, R. (1999). *Sleight of mouth: The magic of conversational belief change.* Capitola, CA: Meta Publications.

Gordon, D., & Dawes, G. (2004). *Modeling: A brief introduction.* http://experiential-dynamics. org/index2.htm.

O'Connor, J., & Seymour, J. (1990). *Introducing NLP: Neurolinguistic programming: Psychological skills for understanding and influencing people.* London/San Francisco: Thorsons/ HarperCollins.

17

Making Decisions

Reaching Consensus in Team Meetings

Michael Ben-Avie, Trudy Raschkind Steinfeld, and James P. Comer

One of the School Development Program's (SDP) guiding principles is that decisions are made by consensus. But what exactly is consensus, and how does one reach it? This chapter contrasts consensus decision making with voting, and explains how reaching consensus in SDP schools translates into increasingly appropriate action steps supported by continuously improving relationships between team members. Strategies are included to help group leaders during the process.

> **consensus** . . . [from the Latin *consentire* . . . to feel together, to agree—related to consent] . . . harmony, cooperation, or sympathy [especially] in different parts of an organism . . . group solidarity in sentiment and belief . . . collective opinion: the judgment arrived at by most of those concerned . . . .
>
> —*Webster's Third New International Dictionary*

CONSENSUS DECISION MAKING IS AN ONGOING PROCESS

In School Development Program (SDP) teams, subcommittees, and classrooms, many important decisions are made by consensus. Groups strive to "find," "achieve," and "reach" consensus. Spoken of in this way, the word consensus sounds like a thing or a place. So it is useful to remember that consensus is actually the result of a process that takes place between people.

Groups should make an effort to monitor that process. The quality of their interactions will strengthen or weaken any group's ability to make decisions and take actions in the future. Before there can be a collective opinion, there must first be a respectful process of gathering all the individual opinions. Then there must be a respectful process of discussing, evaluating, combining, and choosing among them. It is also worth noting that any decision reached through consensus is actually only a temporary decision that will be reassessed whenever necessary.

SDP school communities receive ongoing training and support from national and local facilitators in the most effective and respectful ways to interact. Because they become skilled at thinking about their own interactions as well as the things they're discussing, SDP teams and subcommittees can truly say that consensus is one of their guiding principles.

THE DIFFERENCE BETWEEN VOTING AND CONSENSUS: DIGITAL VERSUS ANALOGUE

The chief alternative way school groups make decisions is by voting. Any situation in which there are only two options—like the on and off positions of a light switch—is called a "digital" situation (Bateson, 1972/2000; O'Connor & Seymour, 1990). Voting, which requires approval or disapproval of a proposal, is therefore digital. Offering alternatives is often seen as complicating, confusing, or even obstructing the voting process. The voter faces a forced choice, and the results can even be tabulated mechanically.

When votes are taken in schools, the difference in real (and perceived) power and authority between members of the school community causes some individuals to feel they do not have the status, the right, or the ability to speak out about certain proposals. This situation, in which some people have (or are perceived to have) all the power and others have (or are perceived to have) none, is also digital.

In addition, the digital quality of voting produces the following drawbacks:

- Many people vote, but typically only a few people select the option to be voted on.
- Those for and against the option limit their time and energy to thinking about ways to get support for their side.
- People focus on the option presented and limit their thinking about what is needed and possible.
- Because the choice seems simple (it's either yes or no, after all), the vote may be taken before the voters have a chance to fully examine the option.
- There are winners and losers, and the losers may become disaffected from further participation or may be angry enough to try to undermine the outcome determined by the vote.

By contrast, a situation in which there is a spectrum (a continuum) of options is called an "analogue" situation (Bateson, 1972/2000; O'Connor & Seymour, 1990). It is continuously variable (even if that variability is between two limits), like the dimmer switch on a light fixture or (if you like even more choice) like a high-tech control panel for lighting and sound, with a full array of levers and dials that can create an almost infinite variety of options between nothing at all and everything, full blast, at once.

The consensus process, therefore, is analogue. Any manageable number of options may be on the table. The options are considered, and combined or selected until all participants feel well-represented and are clear that the students will be well-served by the decision. A type of voting (polling or asking or choosing) is the formal last step of the consensus process, but actually this polling occurs throughout the process as (1) more and more people indicate clearly that they agree with what is being discussed, and (2) fewer and fewer people offer objections while clearly staying engaged in the discussion.

The analogue quality of the consensus process also produces the following benefits:

- Any real or perceived power differential is parked outside the meeting room because group members are required to engage in the process and are supported by facilitators as they develop skills for engaging appropriately.
- The number of people welcome to put options on the table equals the number of people involved in the final choice.
- More than one opinion or option is welcome from each person, so no one needs to back or be backed into a corner defending a single idea.
- People are stimulated to make suggestions about anything that already is or might be on the table.
- The decision-making process opens up to include input from as many people as can contribute to the best possible decision.
- The process continues until the options are fully examined.
- There is no formal choosing until virtually everyone can agree at least to give the most-favored option a real-world try.
- The option chosen is monitored as it is put into practice and will be reassessed as needed, not according to some preset calendar.

THE CONSENSUS PROCESS ENLARGES THE SCHOOL COMMUNITY

Whereas the voting process is inherently exclusive, whittling choices down to a single one, the consensus process is inherently inclusive because it brings not only more ideas but also more people into the life of the school. In order to discover the best ways to meet students' needs, group members reach out to others in and beyond the school. Each person has many contacts, any of whom could be important.

Suppose, for example, that each person in a 10-person group reaches out to 2 people outside the school (for example, parents in other schools, former college professors, business associates, the community service teacher in a local high school, a local newspaper reporter or editor, a librarian, the owner of a computer store or supermarket, an administrator or worker at a hospital). Each group member requests information, ideas, and/or support for the same project. Then suppose that 3 of those 20 people reach out to 2 more people in their own networks and suggest that they get in touch with the members of the original group. Now there are 26 additional people who are actual or potential sources of information and support.

Now multiply these sources times several projects under discussion. The potential to involve additional caring adults is obviously very great.

Schools can encourage an ongoing relationship with these people. Their names, titles, affiliations, contact numbers, and the information and/or service they provided (or could provide in the future) to the group members can easily be kept in a database, now that computers are widely available in schools. How hard could it be to keep them posted by e-mail, letting them know how appreciated their input has been and the ongoing outcomes of the program that was shaped in part by their input?

Once they get in the habit of hearing from the group, these new contacts may also begin to think of the group when something interesting crosses their desk. They may reach out to their own colleagues as well, who may become involved in the school or in another school, and so the benefits may spread from school to school. In this way, the consensus process precipitates an ongoing interest in the learning and development of students and their families.

THE CONSENSUS PROCESS STRENGTHENS ATTITUDES AND SKILLS THAT ARE VALUABLE IN ALL ASPECTS OF LIFE

A machine can tabulate votes, but no machine can perform any part of the consensus process, which requires thoughtful communication between members of the group, nonjudgmental observation of other people's cues, a positive attitude, and a commitment to achieving an outcome acceptable to all. The more frequently people engage positively and productively in the process, the more effortless and natural they find it to be.

This also means that they come to accept taking more time to reach decisions. Classic voting often accomplishes a "quick fix," but this shortchanges a group's potential because the focus is on getting something done instead of building the group's skills and capacity while maintaining and strengthening current and future relationships.

SOME STRATEGIES FOR GROUP LEADERS DURING THE CONSENSUS PROCESS

- If the group is having difficulty agreeing about an item, ask the group to put that item into "the parking lot" until a specified time or point in the process.
- Ask the group to tag each interim decision as being "tentative," pending more information or a better idea in the future (up to a specified time). Nothing is permanent until the end.
- Make graphic representations of all options. This stores them for closer, longer observation and reduces the tension of group members who want to make sure they're being heard. It allows easy "cut-and-paste" merging of several parts of different options into a new, composite option.

- When being challenged, or when feeling like challenging another person (two situations in which relationships might suffer), make meta-comments about the self (self-commentary as if one were a resourceful observer). For example,
    "I hear your objection. I can't give you a response right now, though. I need to think about this. I'll get back to it again *[in a specified time]*."
    "I don't know why I'm responding negatively. . . . I seem to have an objection, even though I can't put my finger on it right now. I'd like to think about it."

Consensus is not time bound and thus allows for a decision to be altered in order to reach the desired goal.

REFERENCES

Bateson, G. (1972/2000). *Steps to an ecology of mind.* Chicago: University of Chicago Press.

O'Connor, J., & Seymour, J. (1990). *Introducing NLP: Neurolinguistic programming— Psychological skills for understanding and influencing people.* London/San Francisco: Thorsons/HarperCollins.

READ MORE ABOUT . . .

To read more about how SDP teaches people to become skilled at thinking about their own interactions, see "A Team Approach to Educational Change," Chapter 10 in *Six Pathways to Healthy Child Development and Academic Success: The Field Guide to Comer Schools in Action* in this series.

18

The School Development Program Implementation Life Cycle

A Guide for Planned Change

Edward T. Joyner

Changing systems as complex as schools takes time. School communities that implement the Comer Process dedicate years to reforming their schools. The School Development Program (SDP) knows from experience that deep, meaningful reform requires more than a quick fix. SDP life cycle guides school communities in their initial five to six years of implementing the Comer Process, after which a renewal phase begins.

SDP also helps school communities to understand that meaningful educational change—change that will impact the lifepaths of children and youth—occurs only when all parts of the system are aligned for this purpose. SDP's action strategies are based on three simple propositions: (1) All school activities should promote holistic student development by improving teaching and learning, (2) school structures should be organized to help achieve this central purpose of schooling, and (3) large-scale educational change cannot happen without the simultaneous transformation of all the substructures (e.g., subcommittees, grade-level groups) that constitute the larger school. If substructures work at odds with one another, there will be a breakdown in implementing any change process. SDP is the umbrella under which all the initiatives within the school community are coordinated and provided with direction.

BEING AN AGENT FOR PLANNED CHANGE

I have always been fascinated with change. At a very young age, I became aware of the changes that occur in nature when I would help my father plant the garden to raise food to feed our family. The entire family pitched in to prepare the soil, to seed, and to water the plants. My father helped me to understand that preparation, planting, watering, fertilizing, and weeding were necessary if we wanted to harvest the corn, tomatoes, cucumbers, collard greens, and squash that helped to supplement the limited amount of food that he and my mother could buy with the minimum wages from their seasonal work in a small southern town. Natural change was all around me.

As I grew older and more sophisticated, I became aware of social change. As a child of the 1960s, I witnessed and participated in the civil rights movement. I saw our nation use the democratic process to move closer to its idea of *E pluribus Unum*. And even though we are not there yet, there have been lessons learned that can serve us as we move closer to the vision of the founding fathers and mothers.

Planned social change must be flexible and adaptable to unforeseen changes in the environment. This means that social change is not linear and must anticipate some chaos. It must constantly sense the environment and acquire the data needed to stay the course or even change the course if necessary. This is a paradox that all students of change must accept.

A change life cycle has to be flexible and adaptable to the various environments that schools and school systems must contend with—but it also must contain the tasks set down in manageable units of time that will lead to goal completion. Each goal completed will require the creation and pursuit of another goal. Because of the nature of human social systems, we will never achieve perfection, but we must constantly pursue it. Here we have another paradox because we must think in terms of immediate tasks and goals while seeing the larger picture, and also realize that good and noble work will remain even after we are no longer around to do it. It is pursuit of worthy aims with our best laid plans that will lead us to noble ends and new beginnings. Robert Burns has taught us a valuable lesson about "best laid plans," so we must have contingencies for plans going awry.

THE SDP IMPLEMENTATION LIFE CYCLE

Both the natural and social changes that I studied as a child and adult have served as the frame of reference that I used to develop the School Development Program (SDP) Implementation Life Cycle. I believe that both natural and social change occurs and can be understood in terms of stages. Each stage must build the momentum for transition to the next one. The stages should not necessarily be seen as discrete, although they may appear that way after the fact.

SDP's 35 years of experience has shown that there are five stages in changing the complex system that is a school. We call these five stages the SDP Implementation Life Cycle. Each stage has a recommended time frame. The stages are planning and preparation, foundation building, transformation, institutionalization, and renewal.

The life cycle is a blueprint for making such structural changes as creating a schoolwide plan that is comprehensive and purposeful, designing ways to measure how the school is improving students' learning and development, and aligning the curriculum with instruction and assessment.

STAGE ONE: PLANNING AND PREPARATION (SIX MONTHS TO ONE YEAR)

Overview of Stage One: Planning and Preparation

- Develop knowledge of process.
- Develop management structures.
- Assign roles and responsibilities.
- Examine the intent of every preexisting school initiative and then use SDP to integrate all the initiatives, thereby creating a unified approach to promoting students' learning and development.
- Use the SDP Implementation Life Cycle to assess movement toward faithful replication.

This stage allows critical stakeholders in the schools to become knowledgeable about the Comer Process, develop the integrative management structures that will create an implementation plan for the schools and partner institution(s), and select participants to attend training at Yale University at the end of the year.

Action Steps

1. Vote by school board to use SDP as the vehicle for school reform.

2. Appoint a district facilitator to oversee program implementation.

3. Form a District Planning Team that is representative of critical stakeholders within the system of education.

4. Commit to use the guiding principles of the Comer Process.

5. Commit to improve and support teaching, thereby facilitating the holistic development of children and youth.

6. Representatives of all stakeholder groups demonstrate collective ownership of the change process.

7. Select a team of representative stakeholders to attend training at Yale.

Outcomes

1. A partnership agreement signed by the leaders of participating groups that outlines roles, rules, and responsibilities.

2. A multiple-year comprehensive plan for implementation that integrates all key school initiatives.

3. A multiple-year strategic plan that details the transformation process at the school level.

4. A program evaluation plan.

5. A baseline description of student characteristics (e.g., academic achievement, social class, attendance rates, social behavior patterns, community demographics). If appropriate, a description of staff characteristics (e.g., years in service, educational attainment, ethnicity).

6. A plan document that details specific action steps for implementation, assigns responsibilities and due dates for completion of specific activities, and identifies evidence to be collected regarding anticipated outcomes.

STAGE TWO: FOUNDATION BUILDING (ONE TO TWO YEARS)

Overview of Stage Two: Foundation Building

- Create three teams and subcommittees to support three operations at the school.
- Integrate guiding principles into school culture.
- Use SDP instrumentation to monitor program implementation.
- Create appropriate staff development activities using internal and external resources.
- Establish the nine program elements in schools and in the networks that support program implementation in the schools (e.g., school district central office, steering committee).
- Balance curriculum and intensify academic focus.
- Use six pathways to improve school's developmental focus.
- Develop public relations campaign to build community awareness of SDP.

The District Planning Team creates an interdepartmental team of central office administrators and staff to support implementation in the schools. School staff participate in professional development and initiate the nine elements of the Comer Process at their schools. School staff work with parents to identify ways that parents can support the home-school collaboration. Parents support the process at the school by attending major school events, volunteering during the school day to support academic and social programs, and serving on the School Planning and Management Team (SPMT) to help shape school policy.

Action Steps

1. A team is sent to national SDP leadership training sessions 101 and 102 (conducted several months apart).

2. The district has a formal protocol in place to monitor implementation.

3. The District Steering Committee meets at least three times a year. The committee tracks and analyzes data for the SDP schools.

4. Each participating school forms an SPMT that is representative of all groups in the school community (e.g., administrators, instructional and noninstructional staff, parents, community representatives, and students, when appropriate). The agenda is reflective of the school's mission to provide quality instruction and to promote youth development.

5. Staff development is provided that is sufficient to address the academic and psychosocial needs of the students in the school and/or district.

6. Participating schools identify members of the Student and Staff Support Team (SSST).

7. The SSST addresses individual student developmental needs and global issues that concern the school community.

8. All parents receive an orientation to SDP and its Parent Team component.

9. At participating schools, existing parent groups are identified, and an assessment is conducted to determine readiness for forming SDP's Parent Team. It may be preferable to strengthen the existing parent group(s) to become the SDP Parent Team rather than forming another team. If another team is formed, then the roles of each team need to be thoughtfully clarified.

10. Comer school facilitators are appointed and trained by Yale SDP staff. They consult with an SDP implementation coordinator on an ongoing basis.

11. Team members, the whole staff, and parents participate in ongoing training about SDP's approach to school reform and child development.

12. Principals and other administrators attend SDP's Principals' Academy at Yale University.

13. Baseline data are collected on each participating school's demographics (e.g., student achievement, student and staff attendance, suspension rates, special education referrals, parent participation).

14. Participating schools engage in a process of self-assessment in the areas of school climate, academic press, and the degree to which elements of SDP are present in the school. They may use such instruments as SDP's climate surveys, the Process Documentation Inventory (PDI), School Implementation Questionnaire (SIQA), or a similar assessment procedure. They use the assessment to modify their school plan, if needed.

15. A school calendar is developed that indicates the dates of both social and academic events and includes school, parent, and district activities.

16. Schools begin the process of defining, aligning, and assessing the curriculum. Curriculum is aligned with local, state, and national standards as well as with the students' development needs.

17. Teachers start implementing Comer-in-the-Classroom.

18. Standing subcommittees of the SPMT are established and are representative of the staff and parents.

Outcomes

1. District strategic plan

2. Comprehensive School Plan at each school

3. School self-assessment reports

4. District calendar of events

5. School calendar of events

6. Written and aligned curriculum for each content area

7. Staff development plans

8. Annual program evaluation

STAGE THREE: TRANSFORMATION (TWO TO THREE YEARS)

Overview of Stage Three: Transformation

- School culture becomes more child-centered.
- Empirical data drive decisions.
- Guiding principles govern behaviors.
- A developmental focus is evident in all programs and activities.
- Student achievement and personal conduct improves.

This stage marks the beginning of the transformation of the school to an organization that strives for academic excellence and promotes community. The school becomes a learning community that is capable of thoughtful self-examination and correction.

Action Steps

1. New staff and parents receive orientation and training in SDP's approach to the educational change process.

2. The District Steering Committee meets at least three times per year. The Committee tracks and analyzes data for the SDP schools.

3. Schools engage in child-centered planning, creating a Comprehensive School Plan (CSP) that addresses children's needs along the six developmental pathways (physical, cognitive, psychological, language, social, and ethical).

4. Schools use the CSP as a guide for adopting new programs and initiatives.

5. The SPMT assesses and modifies the CSP at regular intervals. The plan is data driven. It is aligned with the goals and initiatives established by the district. It is also aligned with state and national mandates.

6. Staff development is planned and implemented based on the needs identified in the CSP. It also provides opportunities for teachers to improve instruction and deepen their knowledge of the developmental pathways as a framework for improving students' holistic development.

7. Participating schools engage in a process of defining and aligning curriculum, instruction, and assessment congruent with local and state standards.

8. School staff, students, and parents use the three guiding principles of no-fault, consensus, and collaboration.

9. The SSST uses the developmental pathways as a guide for identifying problems and generating solutions.

10. SSST interventions are based on increased sensitivity to the real causes of problems that students and their families face. The SSST seeks to create appropriate, nontraditional interventions for students. Emphasis is placed on preventive strategies that lead to minimizing the number of behavioral and special education referrals.

11. The SSST studies schoolwide issues that impact students' healthy development and learning.

12. Students demonstrate appropriate social skills and share in the responsibility of reforming the school. They take leadership roles in school activities. At the middle and high school level, students are represented on the SPMT.

13. The school climate demonstrates a sense of school spirit, caring, and teamwork. The climate supports members of the school community in taking initiative to promote students' learning and development.

14. Adults and students model responsible citizenship and leadership.

15. Classrooms show evidence of student competence in cooperative learning, use of higher-order thinking skills, and other qualities deemed critical by the community.

16. Schools develop goals and activities that address issues of diversity. Classrooms demonstrate sensitivity to multicultural issues.

17. Teachers apply knowledge of child and youth development in their classroom practice and their use of effective teaching strategies.

18. A significant number of staff and parents have been trained at SDP training events.

19. The principal
    works in a collaborative fashion
    is inclusive of others and their ideas in discussions
    is a facilitative leader and resource developer
    is a strong instructional leader
    monitors the implementation of the curriculum
    interacts with staff, parents, and students in a way that promotes shared
        decision making

20. Schools have developed a public relations strategy that supports their reaching out to community-based organizations, agencies, and universities.

21. Parents are active members of the SPMT, Parent Team, and committees. They volunteer, engage in schoolwide planning, and help make decisions.

22. The Parent Team develops relevant and meaningful activities for parents and the school that enhance student learning and enhance the quality of life for families.

23. The SPMT guides the school in documenting and assessing implementation of the nine elements of the Comer Process. All teams, committees, and grade-level groups use the principles and practices of child development to make all decisions.

24. The school district central office and board of education provide clear support for SDP implementation in schools.

25. Schools use data regularly in decision making.

Outcomes

1. District strategic plan

2. Comprehensive School Plans

3. School self-assessment reports

4. District calendar of events

5. School calendar of events

6. Written curriculum for each content area

7. Staff development plans

8. Annual program evaluation report

STAGE FOUR: INSTITUTIONALIZATION (FOUR TO FIVE YEARS)

Overview of Stage Four: Institutionalization

- The nine elements are standard operating procedure in the school.
- Achievement shows consistent gains.
- Students show continuous improvement in personal behavior.
- There is a clear role for parents and families, working in partnership with educators, to support the academic and personal development of their children.

During this stage, aspects of the program are fine-tuned to meet local needs. The district and schools are less reliant on support from the national SDP office. The more successful schools are used as demonstration sites for visitors. Gains are made in student achievement and other areas measuring school effectiveness.

Action Steps

1. New staff and parents receive orientation and training in SDP's approach to the educational change process.

2. The District Steering Committee meets at least three times a year. The committee tracks and analyzes data for the schools.

3. The Comprehensive School Plan (CSP) is the guiding document for all activities in the school/district.

4. The CSP is assessed and/or modified at least three times per year.

5. The school/district has the capacity to conduct its own training and retraining of staff, relying on less coaching and monitoring from SDP national staff.

6. SDP philosophy and the nine elements of the Comer Process organize all the activities of the school/district on behalf of students' learning and development.

7. Schools are engaged in activities that address children's development along the six developmental pathways.

8. The work of the three management teams, subcommittees, and grade-level teams is clearly child centered and focused on student growth.

9. The teams and subcommittees are fully representative of all of the constituent groups in the school/district.

10. Data are used on a regular basis to inform program and curriculum planning.

11. Assessment shows that the school is functioning at a high level, as evidenced by significant academic and social gains.

12. The district supports schools in the alignment of curriculum with standards and assessment measures.

Outcomes

1. District strategic plan

2. Comprehensive school plans

3. Self-assessment reports

4. School and district calendar of events

5. Written curriculum for each content area

STAGE FIVE: RENEWAL

Overview of Stage Five: Renewal

- Schools compare their implementation practices to the conceptual idea of the SDP model.
- Schools are able to contribute to national dissemination and training for the SDP, by sharing their expertise and experience at regional and national events.

Renewal is the time used by the total staff to compare their implementation of the model with the conceptual ideal. It can be used at any point of implementation when it is necessary to assess replication of the process and make the adjustments needed to achieve the vision of the school, district, or partner institution.

Action Steps

1. New staff and parents receive orientation and training in SDP's approach to the educational change process.

2. Staff receives refresher training on the philosophy that underlies SDP and its Comer Process.

3. There is an effort to renew and rebuild relationships within and outside the school.

4. Data are reviewed to examine trends in achievement, behavior, and school climate.

5. Processes for balancing the curriculum with new standards and/or assessment strategies are refined.

6. Selected administrators, staff, and facilitators are sent to Yale University for refresher training events.

Outcomes

1. District strategic plan

2. Comprehensive school plans

3. School self-assessment reports

4. District calendar of events

5. School calendar of events

6. Written curriculum for each content area

AN INVITATION FOR YOU

I believe that the life cycle is a valuable tool to help you learn and apply the nine elements of SDP. It has broad application, because every project requires planning, preparation, and the building of a foundation to support transformation and the institutionalization of change. For continued progress, most institutional practices must be periodically renewed in order to adapt to environmental changes. Please use our life cycle model in the spirit of SDP and feel free to adapt it to your own needs.

Resources

A: CONSENSUS REMINDER CARD

Todas las decisiones son hechas en el
mejor interés de los niños.

DECISIONES EN CONJUNTO

CONSENSUS

All decisions are made in the best
interests of children.

B: COLLABORATION REMINDER CARD

Todas las decisiones son hechas en el mejor interés de los niños.

COLABORACIÓN

COLLABORATION

All decisions are made in the best interests of children.

C: NO-FAULT REMINDER CARD

Todas las decisiones son hechas en el
mejor interés de los niños.

NO SE CULPA

NO-FAULT

All decisions are made in the best
interests of children.

D: ROLE EXPECTATION CARDS

Group Member (applicable to all members of the team)

- Represent voices of the school community
- Communicate back to the school community or group represented the decisions made by the team
- Communicate the reasons for those decisions
- Be very active on the team and contribute ideas, insights, opinions, and suggestions
- Listen, listen, and listen some more!
- Be willing to support a team decision, even if you do not fully agree with it

Chairperson

- Help create an agenda with input from team members
- Call the meeting to order
- Define the tasks clearly
- Keep the team on task
- Expedite the making of decisions
- Keep discussions focused on children and the agenda items

Principal/Administrator

- Help set up meeting locations and times
- Ensure that information is distributed as needed
- Help members see the "big picture" (school board issues, goals, state and district mandates, etc.)
- Help define and clarify parameters of the team's power and responsibility
- Help identify issues that might relate to the principal, superintendent, budget, board policy, school law, etc.
- Help make the meetings child centered

Facilitator

- Support the chairperson and the principal by helping the team with its process (relationship) issues
- Listen actively
- Help everyone participate
- Help everyone be heard
- Clarify confusion or differences by paraphrasing what is heard
- Help differences to be discussed and resolved
- Support and ensure that information summarized by the reporter or notetaker is communicated to other groups and teams

Notetaker (Recorder)

- Record minutes of the meeting
- List the key decisions made by the team
- Record who will do what and when
- Provide copies of minutes for the entire school community
- Maintain a file of the minutes for each meeting

Timekeeper

- Let the team members know when they are at midpoint in time on an agenda item
- Let the team know when five minutes are left and when one minute is left
- Negotiate for more time if it is needed
- Help the team begin and end on time, or negotiate to change time frame

Reporter

- Discuss with the team the notes taken by the notetaker
- Decide with the team the most important or relevant information to report out
- Summarize the information and any key decisions made that other groups might need to know
- Stand up and deliver the information to the larger group (e.g., at a training event)

Process Observer

- Take notes on behaviors seen that help or hinder the tasks and relationships
- Provide nonjudgmental feedback about observed behaviors at the end of the meeting or the beginning of the next meeting
- Help the team have a dialogue on its effectiveness (may sometimes be done in conjunction with the facilitator)

Index

**CORWIN
PRESS**

The Corwin Press logo—a raven striding across an open book—represents the union of courage and learning. Corwin Press is committed to improving education for all learners by publishing books and other professional development resources for those serving the field of K–12 education. By providing practical, hands-on materials, Corwin Press continues to carry out the promise of its motto: **"Helping Educators Do Their Work Better."**